"This is the book all Brigid devotees and en[...] about. *Brigid's Light* is a bubbling cauldron of wisdom and inspiration, and it absolutely belongs on your shelf. I'm sure I'll be coming back to this one for decades to come."

—Tess Whitehurst, author of *You Are Magical* and *Holistic Energy Magic*

"Introducing us to the beloved goddess, Brigid, in her different guises, *Brigid's Light* is a truly special, appropriately illuminating, and richly diverse collection of writings from some of the most respected figures in contemporary witchcraft and spirituality. Trusted hands—including those of Judika Illes and Byron Ballard—shine a light on the many facets of this ever-inspirational Celtic deity, guiding us into her realm through the medium of spells, poetry, recipes, crafting, personal reflections, rituals, and much more besides. This sparkling anthology is a gift, both to Brigid and to the reader. Nurture your inner fire with this book, and tune in to Brigid's bright energy, not only at Imbolc, but all the year round."

—Zoë Howe, author of *Witchful Thinking*

"Brigid was the first goddess that had a direct impact on how my life unfolded. I can also see her light and her hand at work throughout the world in many individuals and communities today. *Brigid's Light* is more than an excellent anthology; it is an act of healing and the creation of a community of practice. Divine beings are vast and beyond the comprehension of any single human being. However, when you bring together the thoughts, experiences, and insight of many people such as is present in this book, you begin to get a glimmer of Brigid's majesty and her nature. If you are called by her, you will find both confirmation and challenges in this book, and that is her way."

—Ivo Dominguez Jr. author of *The Four Elements of the Wise*

BRIGID'S LIGHT

Tending the Ancestral Flame of the Beloved Celtic Goddess

EDITED BY CAIRELLE CROW AND LAURA LOUELLA

WEISER BOOKS

This edition first published in 2022 by Weiser Books, an imprint of

Red Wheel/Weiser, LLC
With offices at:
65 Parker Street, Suite 7
Newburyport, MA 01950
www.redwheelweiser.com

ISBN: 978-1-57863-769-0

Library of Congress Cataloging-in-Publication Data available upon request.

Cover design by Kathryn Sky-Peck
Cover art *Brighde*, 2000 © Stuart Littlejohn
Interior by Deborah Dutton
Typeset in Adobe Garamond Pro, Frutiger LT Std, Chalet Comprime and Morpheus

Printed in the United States of America
IBI

10 9 8 7 6 5 4 3 2 1

DEDICATION

To Brigid, goddess, saint, and traveling companion,
and to the memory of the ancestors who crossed oceans
and continents, carrying her with them.

Contents

Part III: Ritual Practices and Prayers

Part IV: Goddess of Hearth and Home

Part V: Mothers and Daughters

Part VI: The Circle of Life and Death

Foreword

Welcome to *Brigid's Light*, an anthology dedicated to Brigid, a multifaceted sacred being whose forms include an extremely beloved goddess and saint. The earliest documentation of Brigid is in Ireland. She appears in the *Book of Invasions*, a mythic history of Ireland that was formalized in the 11th and 12th centuries, but was drawn from much earlier oral and written sources. Archaeological and etymological evidence indicates that her presence was once widespread throughout the British Isles and likely to have been quite ancient.

Brigid is a goddess of artisanry, poetry, smithcraft, healing, fertility, midwifery, prosperity, and protection. Her name is typically interpreted as referencing fire; her mythos includes unusual, sacred flames, sometimes emanating from her own head or body. But Brigid is a water goddess as well, associated with numerous holy wells and springs throughout the British Isles.

Brigid is a complex goddess, simultaneously ancient and modern. The *Book of Invasions* credits her with inventing the art of keening—vocalized lamenting of the dead that expresses the rawest, most primal grief. While not a spirit of death, Brigid is the goddess of mourners and mourning. As a goddess of craftsmanship, she is also associated with modern technology, as well as with traditional crafts.

Irish mythology identifies Brigid as a member of the *Tuatha Dé Danann*, the spirits who would evolve into the *Sidhe* or *Shee*—the Irish fairies or *fae*. Following Ireland's conversion to Christianity, most female members of this pantheon were, at best, demoted to fairy queens. Brigid is the exception. She was able to make the transition to Christianity and retained her reputation as a benevolent holy being, albeit in a different form.

Brigid is a shapeshifter. As a goddess, she takes many forms: as a woman of various ages from girl to crone, as a serpent, as a pillar of fire, and as a woman with flames emanating from her head. Sometimes she appears as a single being, but she may also take the form of a triplicity, or as three sisters. Brigid seems able to take on the spiritual characteristics most needed and most accessible to her devotees.

Depending on interpretation and personal belief, Brigid of Kildare may or may not be the goddess in the guise of a Christian saint. Some believe that the goddess evolved into the saint or accepted the mask of the saint, perhaps to remain close to her devotees. With the banishing of Paganism, most Irish deities were suppressed, forgotten, or demonized. Brigid, however, transitioned to sainthood.

Others, however, believe that Saint Brigid is *not* the goddess in disguise, but an actual, historical woman, perhaps the last priestess of the goddess who, having converted to Christianity, was able to integrate her beliefs in a way that remained true to her past and present. Some theorize that, as part of their ritual practice, Brigid's priestesses adopted her name, hence the shared name of saint and goddess. Even today, as you will see in these pages, modern practitioners adopt Brigid's name in order to honor her, but also to establish their spiritual connections with her and perhaps to allow her power and holiness to radiate through them.

Brigid the goddess and Brigid the saint share more than their names, however. Their feast days, constituencies, interests, and iconology are close to identical. Beyond the identity of the saint as a Christian and the identity of her precursor as Pagan, the boundaries between the two can be nebulous. Legends of the saint have crept into the goddess's mythology and vice versa. Saint Brigid has dominion over domestic animals like pigs and cows. Many of her legends reference the preparation of food and beer, often produced in a miraculous fashion, and always preternaturally delicious.

Brigid may also manifest in other sacred guises. In the 18th century, she appears to have accompanied the Irish Brigade to what is now Haiti, where she may have jumped ship and evolved into the Vodou spirit (*lwa*) Maman Brigitte or Madame Brigitte, although this is currently controversial and fiercely debated.

Brigid's impact continues to resonate. Her influence has consistently increased through the ages, rather than the reverse. Brigid accompanied her Celtic devotees as they traveled around the globe, and she is now loved by people worldwide and not only by those of Celtic origin. Her constituency has broadened and diversified exponentially and continues to do so. *Brigid's Light* explores that impact.

Editors Cairelle Crow and Laura Louella have gathered together a brilliant panorama of contributions for your reading pleasure and spiritual insight. Brigid in her guise as a goddess of creativity is well represented. The contributors to this anthology are from many walks of life and from various spiritual traditions. They come mostly from outside the places that are traditionally considered Brigid's heartland, and they express her modern, vital, active presence in their lives. Some are well-known authors; others are published here for the first time. But all their contributions—whether prose, poetry, art, or recipes—are heartfelt and suffused with love of Brigid.

May Brigid's bright blessings shine upon you.

Judika Illes, author of the *Encyclopedia of Spirits*
and the *Encyclopedia of Mystics, Saints, and Sages*

Introduction

The immigrant's heart marches to the beat of two quite different drums, one from the old homeland and the other from the new. The immigrant has to bridge these two worlds, living comfortably in the new and bringing the best of his or her ancient identity and heritage to bear on life in an adopted homeland.

Mary McAleese, President of Ireland, 1997–2011

For those who know her, Brigid is a divine enigma. Her oldest guise of dawn goddess is shrouded in the mists, certain knowledge of her lost to a time when the mysteries and lore of the Celtic peoples were passed on through storytelling. As a saint, she is revered for miracles; as a historical person, her existence is questioned by scholars. Yet she perseveres. In her modern form, she greets us with two faces—one as goddess and one as saint. She bridges the spiritual chasm between Christianity and Paganism with aplomb and grace as she leads people to common ground. She offers to those who seek her the blessings of healing, creativity, inspiration, protection, and more. Many have questions about her that can be challenging to answer, and there is much we cannot know for sure. But despite these uncertainties, she is venerated around the world by millions.

Brigid is first documented in the folklore, mythology, and spiritual traditions of the Celtic nations of Scotland, Ireland, Wales, Cornwall, the Isle of Man, and Brittany, as well as in England, where she is revered at numerous sacred sites. As a pre-Christian triple goddess of Ireland, Brigid is an object of reverence over a wide expanse of northwestern Europe, and her traditions were carried by traveling devotees to the remotest reaches of the earth. She is now part and parcel of the spiritual practices of many diverse peoples.

Today, Brigid has an extensive and faithful following of devotees around the world. This is not surprising, as emigration forms much of the modern history of the Celtic peoples. Over the last few centuries, immigrants from every Celtic nation have traveled to the far corners of the world, whether to escape economic hardship, to flee religious and political oppression, or simply because of an appetite for adventure. It has been estimated that there may be as many as seventy million people of Irish descent around the world today, with a further twenty million claiming Scottish ancestry. There are also several million of Welsh, Breton, and Cornish ancestry scattered around the Americas and Australia. Overall, there are well over 100 million people worldwide who can claim an ancestral connection to the Celtic lands including an estimated three and a half million English who immigrated to the United States after 1776.

Immigrants from Celtic lands, many of whom were indentured servants, carried Brigid with them to places like British North America, Australia, and the British West Indies, in particular Barbados, Jamaica, and the Leeward Islands. It was in the Caribbean that many believe Saint Brigid became syncretized with the Haitian Vodou *lwa* (spirit) Maman Brigitte, mingling with traditional beliefs that originated in Africa. From there, worship of the goddess/saint traveled to the United States, where she is now much venerated, especially in New Orleans. Others disagree, maintaining that, although their names are similar, Maman Brigitte is actually syncretized with Mary Magdalene and has nothing to do with Saint Brigid. Whichever argument you accept, the fact that Brigid is even considered to have a connection to a deity belonging to a completely separate spiritual tradition speaks to her wide influence and appeal.

These immigrants all brought their cultural identity and traditions with them to a new homeland. As they intermarried with those from other places and traditions, their culture and beliefs were fused into an amalgamation of past and present, a mosaic of old and new, in a true portrayal of America's great melting pot and a reflection of our multicultural world. Author Caitlin Matthews points out wonderful instances of what she calls "double-decker beliefs" that are scattered throughout folk traditions worldwide. "The Russians have a good word for this kind of thing," she tells us, "naming it *dvoverie* or 'double-belonging,' a word originally coined to cover those who had an earlier belief running alongside a later one. Wherever a newer tradition has come into a country, the older one doesn't just die or go away, but becomes fused with the newer one, so that the traditional continuity can be enjoyed by us all" (*Soundings* blog, 2013).

Thanks to modern-day travel and communications, Brigid's devotees are able to connect with each other and with their ancestral homelands in ways that our forebears could not. This was the case for us. Our discovery of a mutual connection to Brigid came about quite by chance. In a scene reminiscent of a thriller novel, we met on a cold snowy night and traveled many miles together over treacherous icy roads to our destination. During the journey, our conversation turned to our shared spiritual path and to our devotion to Brigid. In that moment, the spark of acquaintance ignited into the flame of a friendship that has grown deep and meaningful—one that is kept flourishing, despite our distance, thanks to technology. In much the same way, people from all over the world share similar connections that bind them to each other and to this remarkable spiritual tradition.

GODDESS AND SAINT

Like other figures in Irish mythology, Brigid is an ancestral goddess very much connected to the land and to water. She is a goddess of the dawn and of fire. The flame is hailed as her standard, as seen in the tale of nineteen priestesses who tended an eternal flame in her name, a tradition that continues today with ritual flame-keeping on a nineteen-day cycle (see Conclusion). Brigid was the first in Irish tradition to perform the ritualized funeral wailing known as "keening." When the shock of her son's death ripped through her, she responded with an initial shriek that set us upon the path of processing our own grief in a way that cleanses (see Part VI). She inspires poets and artists to create. She heals us emotionally and physically. She wraps those in need within her cloak of comfort and protection.

Many believe that Brigid is a modern manifestation of an unnamed primeval deity, and we do see hints of her fiery nature in Indo-European pre-Christian spirituality like that found in the worship of the Roman goddess Vesta and the Greek hearth goddess Hestia. But the name Brigid—which is thought by some to be a modern creation taken from a title meaning "high one" or "exalted one"—does not appear in the historical record before her first appearance in Celtic lands.

A Goddess by Any Other Name . . .

A variety of cultural, religious, and historical influences have created many different spellings of Brigid's name including Brigit, Brighde, Bridget, Brighid, Brigida, Brijit, Brig, Bride, Ffraid, Breet, Brigdu, Bhrida, Brigitte, Brid, Birgitta, Breeshey, and others. She is also known as Mary of the Gael. All are correct.

Many experience this goddess as Saint Brigid of Kildare, an abbess said to have been born in 451 CE in Faughart, County Louth, Ireland. As a Christian saint, she enjoys a rich and storied tradition that has sustained people's faith over nearly two millennia. There are many legends surrounding Saint Brigid's life that lead some scholars to question whether she was a real person. In one of these, Brigid appears as an experienced dairywoman and brewer who is purported to have turned water into beer. In another, her prayers are said to have stilled the wind and rain. In yet another, she persuades the King of Leinster to give her land on which she can build her abbey. When the king agrees that she may have as much land as her cloak will cover, she spreads it out to cover the land as far as the eye can see.

Like the Pagan goddess, Saint Brigid is associated with poetry, smithcraft, healing, protection, and domestic animals. She is known for her generosity to the poor, and many of her miracles relate to healing, hearth and home, and tasks that are typically considered "woman's work." Her Christian feast day falls on February 1st—the same day as the traditional Gaelic festival of Imbolc, sometimes spelled Imbolg, which marks the midway point between winter solstice and spring equinox and is dedicated to the goddess.

Yet many questions about Brigid persist. Who exactly is she? Has the early goddess simply been reinvented time and again over the millennia to become who she is now? Is Saint Brigid merely a convenient hybrid manifestation intended to capture the essence of the Pagan goddess and make Christianity more palatable to recent converts? Or was the saint indeed a living woman whose life stories have taken on characteristics of the goddess's myths and legends?

With Brigid, there seem to be no right or wrong answers to these questions. She is perceived and venerated in different ways by those who follow her. Many accept that goddess and saint are inextricably intertwined, each possessing attributes of the other, and this acceptance has brought about a camaraderie of sorts among various faiths. Devotional acts like flame-keeping often take place within multidenominational groups and across many spiritual traditions. Her devotees share a mutual respect and an understanding that Brigid is simply whoever we need her to be.

Since the revelation of our own mutual devotion to Brigid, we've had many conversations about her history, her mysteries, and her presence in our lives. Unsurprisingly, we are quite aligned in our beliefs and practices. Within our own personal gnosis, Brigid is a triad of sisters—the Sacred Three—with hints of Saint Brigid's legends and miracles threading through the tapestry of our experiences. Brigid is Goddess of the Flame, liminal, born on a threshold at the moment of dawn with fire bursting forth from her head like a halo. She stands with us at the in-between points of our lives, calling us to her so we can learn how to face the moment. She encourages us to look deeply into who we are as women, mothers, friends, and priestesses. She enables us to take stock of where we are and where we are going. By her light, we find our way.

For us, Brigid is a mother goddess embodied in the land and rivers through which she flows, offering her sacred milk as sustenance for our souls. As Lady of the Well, she blesses us with her healing grace throughout our lives, from birth to death. She inspires us and causes our ideas to flow and manifest into beautiful works. She teaches us to speak our truths, and with our words we are empowered. We look to her as a warrior goddess as well—one who stands when it would be easier to sit, who embodies strength and defends the weak and downtrodden, who faces authority and claims the sovereignty that has always been hers.

In this book, we want to share how Brigid expanded our own thinking of who we are as her priestesses and how we experience her in the world. As we began to solicit and compile the contributions for this anthology, we originally thought to keep submissions strictly limited to the Americas and Australia. We quickly realized, however, that we were inhibiting the scope of our beloved goddess. We discovered how widely she has traveled the world, not only through immigration, but also through books, classes, covens and, in these modern times, technology. It quickly became clear that it was not our place to silence anyone by omission. Nor was it our role to change the voice or vision of any of our contributors. In the collection of writings and art found here, we have tried to reflect Brigid's diversity in a wide variety of experiences of her power, a number of unique portrayals of her divinity, and even in different writing styles and spellings of her name.

That is Brigid's way. All are welcome; all are welcomed. We sincerely hope the diversity of authors and artists found here reflects the wide spectrum of people around the world who were guided to the goddess by the light of her vast and loving influence.

We invite you to brew a cup of tea, light a candle, and partake of Brigid as seen through the eyes and hearts of her followers. The works of devotion found here stand as evidence that Brigid is everywhere. We thank you for reading with an appreciation for the variety of traditions and beliefs found across our beautiful world. May the light of her flame always guide you to your highest purpose.

Bright blessings!

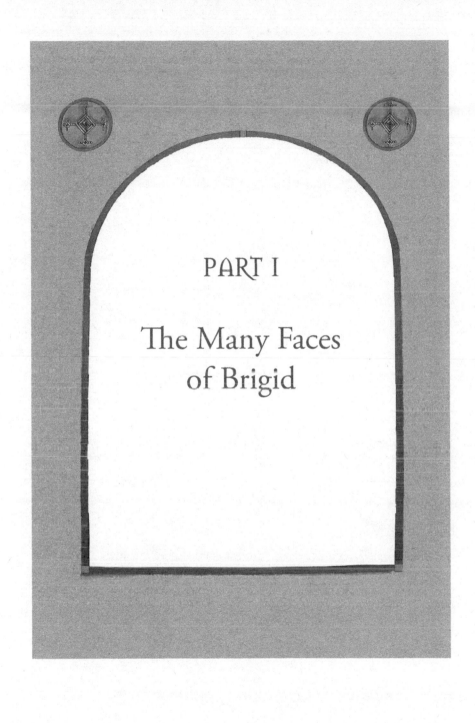

PART I

The Many Faces of Brigid

Celtic Cross

Cairelle Crow

In 1990, a Celtic Cross, hand-carved from Irish marble by Irish hands in County Kilkenny, Ireland, made its way to New Orleans and was erected by the Irish Cultural Society of New Orleans (see Figure 1). This memorial marker stands near the place where, in the early 1800s, Irish immigrant laborers gave their lives while digging the now-filled New Basin Canal. It is a memorial to lost lives. But it is also a testament to the hard work, strength, and tenacity of the Irish who flourished here and who contributed in countless ways to make New Orleans a glorious multicultural gem, world-renowned for music, food, architecture, celebration, and an overall joie de vivre that isn't found anywhere else.

The cross sits in the neutral ground on West End Boulevard and I pass it frequently on my drive to Lake Pontchartrain. Whenever I see it, I think for a moment about two of my own Irish ancestors who journeyed from Ireland to New Orleans in 1851 on the ship *Arlington*. Documents show that they were sick on arrival with "debililty and remit fever" and spent their first days in New Orleans as patients in Charity Hospital. Their decision to cross an ocean in hopes of a better life has resulted in countless descendants born of their six children. At least one of them—myself, a great-great-granddaughter of their daughter Margaret—spreads the beauty and magic of Brigid far and wide.

Did a whisper of Brigid come down to me through the years from this particular Irish grandmother? Maybe. Either way, in my heart, this cross represents love, family, strength, a traveling Brigid, a new life filled with hopes and dreams, and the memories of a faraway place once called home.

Figure 1. Celtic Cross, hand-carved from Irish marble by Irish hands in County Kilkenny, Ireland, brought to New Orleans in 1990 to mark the place where, in the early 1800s, Irish immigrant laborers gave their lives while digging the now-filled New Basin Canal. Photo by Linda L. Minutola.

Sweet Gille Brìghde

Donna Gerrard

Sweet Gille Brìghde
Guide Bird of Bride
Sweet guiding bird
Where your call is heard
Sailors follow what they hear
Knowing a safe shore is near

Sweet Gille Brìghde
Guide Bird of Bride
"Bi glic" be wise
Come your piping cries
Mariners hear you warn
Of the oncoming storm

Sweet Gille Brìghde
Guide Bird of Bride
"Hi glic" take care
You call through the air
Fishermen hear your cry
Knowing home they must hie

Sweet Gille Brìghde
Guide Bird of Bride
Companion of Brigantia
Our Lady of Alba
Your sweet trusty song
Leads me to where I belong

She Laid Her Hand Upon My Head

H. Byron Ballard

For decades now, I have been a priestess to Inanna, the Sumerian goddess of heaven and earth. I knew little about her when she claimed me, but I versed myself in all there was to know through books and, later, through scholarship available on the Internet. But I mostly learned through asking—through waking visions and sleeping dreams, on bright hillsides and in the womb-caves of the planet. We forged a good, if lopsided, relationship. I served her, but there was no temple here and her homeland wasn't accessible to me. So I became her temple and listened to her voice. I sang her songs and danced as I poured the libation every New Moon.

This continued until my country declared war on hers. One of her many faces is that of the warrior and she turned that face toward me, only for moments, and then turned away. At last—on the day that an earthquake shook the town of Bam, killing so many people—she came to me in a dream, standing on my chest and looking at me from a great and terrible height.

"You cannot serve me now. I release you to your own people."

She was gone. I was bereft.

We were a few days past Winter Solstice and looking toward a cultural New Year. Like many Pagans, I celebrate the start of the new year at the end of October. I moped around until the beginning of January and began to plan for Imbolc. I was creating public rituals for the community in those days before we formed the Mother Grove Goddess Temple, and Imbolc had always been a favorite. The rising energy and the chance to celebrate together at the edge of the winter's darkness made—and still makes—that holy day very special indeed.

Turning to my *Carmina Gadelica*, I read everything in that fat volume about Saint Brigid or Bridey. Some of it felt too Catholic and contrived for me, while some still bore a whiff of what once was. Searching past the hagiography and the saint's tales, I thought that, if I squinted and held my breath, I could just about make out the shape of the older figure bending at her forge or carrying a lamb. The more I peered at the shadowy figure behind the saint, the closer I came to understanding what I was seeing. Sitting with my *Carmina* at my desk, I started to tear away layers from the prayers and incantations. With my limited knowledge of Old Irish and of Scots, I felt inside for the correct rhythm of this elusive gold-red woman. I repeated lines and built on lines, focusing on triads and threnodies. My throat found the rasp and call of keening. Exhausted with the pursuit, I put my head back and slept.

I woke to a cool palm on my forehead and a gentle humming sort of sound—not quite a song, but intentional and inviting. I kept my eyes closed and waited, breathing in the scent of fresh-mown hay and, curiously, the smell of sweet, dark beer. The hand moved to the top of my head and was joined by another hand. I wanted to open my eyes and see what was going on, but I couldn't, because I was dreaming. Other voices took up the sound and I felt myself surrounded by women. The smells became more complex. I sensed burning tallow and rain on fresh-turned soil, turnip greens cooking, and—I don't think I was mistaken—sheep droppings.

The humming sound continued and the one whose hands were on my head spoke at last. She spoke in what I now know to be Old Irish and in the three-part rhythmic cadence that I'd studied that day. The poem was a song of welcome and of returning. In it, a prodigal had returned in grief, but also in power. This sojourner in a far land was known to the gathered women and had been missed and remembered. There were hands on my shoulders then, and hands that took up my own hands and raised me from my computer chair, leading me in a dance of homecoming. For I was the prodigal, the traveler returning from distant lands; my ancestors had found me as I wandered toward home.

It took a little longer for me to become an official dedicant of the goddess, because that required me to think about my service to Inanna. So I never became Brigid's priestess. A few years later, I renewed my vows as a priestess of Inanna, resuming the pouring of New Moon libations, the dance, the service.

My service to Brigid is entirely different. She stands with my people, those insistent ancestors who fled their homes in famine, fire, and war, and settled in this new place. I keep her holy day and I tell her stories. She is more teacher and sister than Great Queen, and my work with her is cozier, more practical, and, frankly, more fulfilling. I have been to her fire temple in Kildare, where I made the second part of my dedication. I sing her songs and teach her lore.

And when I tie clouties at her blessed spring, I can still hear the voices around me, softly raising me up and welcoming me home.

Brigid Dark and Bright

H. Byron Ballard, adapted from Carmichael

In the steep and common path of our calling,
Be it easy or uneasy to our flesh,
Be it dark or bright for us to follow,
May your perfect guidance be upon us.
Brigid of the Forge, be thou a shield to us!
Brigid of the Fold, be thou our shepherd and our healer!
In each secret thought our minds may weave, Brigid of the Loom,
    give us sweet clarity.
In our grief or pain or sadness,
Brigid of the Well, heal us, strengthen us, stand with your mighty
    shoulder near to ours.
And in our joys and in our bliss, Brigid of the Hearth, Keeper of the
    Bread Plate, Maker of Beer,
Dance with us as we waken the great round garden of the world.

The Goddess Returns to Her Temple

Sandra Román

I felt sure it was the spirit of Dorothy Kerin who broke my computer. Above my screen, I'd gently displayed the biography of that woman who had become a healer after returning from the dead. It was just a small touch, but it was enough to make the screen suddenly go black and not turn on again. There weren't any other computers at the bookshop that could access the catalog software, so for at least a week, I wasn't able to work.

On that beautiful and sunny day, I began to feel that I was wasting my time working nonstop. I didn't get up from my seat to eat or to go to the toilet, yet the owner still was not happy with me. I suspected that my employment there was hanging by a subtle thread. But I depended on my meager wage to stay in England and continue my training as a Priestess of Avalon. Otherwise, I would have to return to Argentina.

It didn't make any sense to torment myself with these sad thoughts, so I decided to go out and enjoy the day. I went to the nearby town where there is an outdoor shopping center near an old train station. I loved to walk among the flowers at the plant shop, which was filled with multi-colored begonias and tulips, and the scented air helped to clear my mind. Soon my destiny would be defined and it would be the one that the goddess had chosen. But for now, I was living the moment as a gift the goddess gave me to do something outside my routine.

I asked an assistant about some blocks of clay I found and he told me they were for sale. People usually bought them to create sculptures, he said. They were huge and I thought it would be a great experience to try making a goddess sculpture myself. Why not?

My first challenge was to carry the weight of that huge block of clay. I did it painfully but happily as I embarked on my creative adventure. Next, as I prepared the materials in front of my altar honoring Brigit, I invoked her to guide my inexperienced hands so that they could coax something beautiful from the clay. I lit her flame and heard her words inside me:

Come and drink from my sacred waters
the inspiration you need.
Dive deep into my healing
and infinite transparencies.
Burn yourself in my fire
of beauty,
merging from the heat of my forge,
and leave my temple
transformed into a jewel.
Taste my sacred herbs
to awaken your own medicine.
I am the goddess who feeds your inner fire
with creativity and inspiration.

I took the chalice from the altar to drink the water I had collected from the White Spring, inside her holy cave. I placed my hands on the clay, trying to remember what I had learned in one of the workshops at my first Goddess Conference in Glastonbury. We worked creating balls of clay, modeling only in round shapes, until finally a body of the goddess appeared. The results were similar to ancient archaeological figurines. The clay between my hands seemed to come to life. I imagined the Mother experienced that same wonderful feeling when she created us, her children.

After modeling some shapes that made me feel quite happy, I noticed that I still had a few kilos of clay, enough to manifest my original idea to make a bigger sculpture of Brigit. I wanted to thank and honor her, she whom I invoked when I needed to be inspired and who had cared for me. She always responds to me, making me feel her blissful presence. I got to work and lost myself in that timeless creative energy. I have never felt anything like it since. It was a magical and healing experience.

I find it difficult to explain with words what I felt as I watched the image of the goddess emerge. I believe she entered me, flooding me with an energy that went through me like a balm to finally manifest her form through my hands.

As I immersed myself in the task of sculpting the image, my concerns seemed to melt away. I finished reading the biography of Dorothy Kerin—which I had been working on adding to the bookstore catalog—trying to find out how a devout Christian could relate to a Pagan goddess and how she had become her messenger from the beyond. Surely, in the spirit world, there are no differences between religions. Brigit radiates her healing energies to all who offer their lives in the service of healing and comforting the vulnerable.

I returned to my work when my computer was repaired, but I knew I could not continue there for much longer. The money they paid me was not enough and I could not get a better job. So I came to know that my time at Glastonbury was ending and that the goddess now had a new destiny waiting for me in my own land.

I had sold all my possessions in Argentina when I came to settle in Glastonbury, and I now had to take the same path in reverse. I sold what I could and gave the rest to charity shops. But what would I do with the image of the goddess? How could I make sure she would be safe and in a proper place? I held on to the sculpture, hoping to donate it to the Goddess Temple when it opened. We still had not found a suitable location for the temple, however. The priestesses of Avalon were working in temporary temples until a place could be found where they could establish a permanent one.

In Glastonbury's high street, there is a courtyard with many quaint shops that offer quartz, incense, esoteric books, and beautiful materials for rituals and magical practices—a lovely place known as the Glastonbury Experience. The buildings are several hundred years old and some even appear to be from medieval times. Many of us feel that this place is the heart of the community. It is here that a group of volunteers revived the spiritual tradition of Avalon and returned Glastonbury to its role as a pilgrimage center—not only for Christians, but for all beliefs and soul paths.

During my priestess training, I often went to a temple space there called the Bridget Chapel that was open to those who wanted to meditate, pray, or simply enjoy being in silence. The walls had niches that had once housed religious images. The building, which had once belonged to the Abbey, had perhaps been used as a place where pilgrims came to rest. But since it was now open to all religions, no symbols or images of any kind were allowed.

I really loved that place, but I felt a little sad to see it so bereft of its spiritual residents. I felt that, if Brigit were its guardian, there should at least be one image of her displayed inside. My heart raced with a crazy idea. I knew it was not possible. I knew it was not allowed. But I felt within me that the goddess herself was asking me to do it. I could not refuse. The challenge was to do it without anyone noticing me. I was excited about my planned transgression, but I also felt waves of fear creeping through my body.

The courtyard was always crowded during the day and closed at night, so I had no choice but to carry out my operation in broad daylight, in full view of everyone. If I were discovered, it would make for an embarrassing spectacle—or, much worse, maybe they could even send me to jail. I no longer knew how to distinguish between a logical thought and a delusion. Inside my head there was enormous confusion, but my heart knew what the goddess was asking of me and I was not willing to give in.

I looked for a box big enough to hold the sculpture and got a cart that would make it easy for me to move it without damaging it. I passed through the entrance to the crowded courtyard. To make my situation even more ridiculous, the wheels of the cart made a tremendous noise on the old cobblestones. It was impossible to go unnoticed and yet it seemed as if I had become invisible. Nobody saw me. I slipped through the crowd unnoticed. Only when I entered the chapel did I dare to breathe. Thankfully, it was empty.

I don't know where I found the strength I needed to lift the image and place it in one of the niches—or maybe I do. In doing so, I felt that I was returning the goddess to her rightful place, not only in her temple, but also within me. Days later, I said goodbye to Glastonbury with so much pain in my soul, but also with the knowledge that there was a great job as a priestess of the goddess waiting for me in my own country.

More than a year passed before the miracle finally happened. Those who were in charge of Bridget Chapel decided to give it up so that the Library of Avalon could open in the space. Then the Temple of the Goddess could finally open its doors in the space previously occupied by the library. The goddess had claimed and found her place in that courtyard, the present location of the Glastonbury Goddess Temple.

And so, our beloved Bridget, Bridie, Brigid, Brigit, Brígida continues to spread her light of wisdom, healing, love, and transformation from there as Lady of Avalon. When I recall my little adventure with her, I feel her lovely words resonating within me once again.

I am the Goddess who feeds your inner fire.
I am Brigit, the Golden One.
Do not let my flame be extinguished
Nor let it be taken away
From the home of your heart.

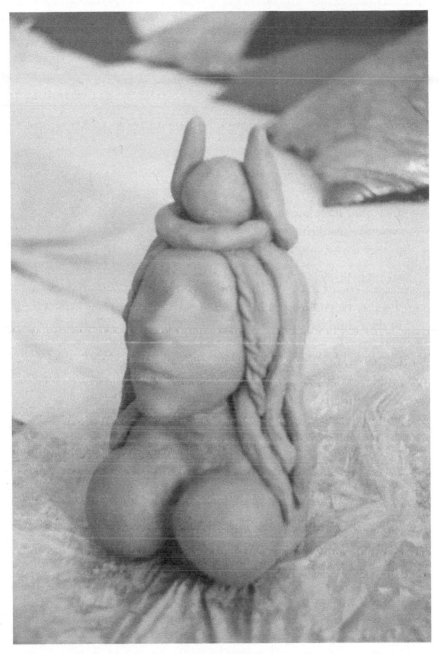

Figure 2. The Goddess Brigit, molded and sculpted in clay, as envisioned by the artist. Photo by Sandra Román.

Brigit in Canada

Mael Brigde

you were there
in Leinster and Uist
in County Dublin

they must have known you
were you invoked
as they curled inside their mothers

awaiting birth

did they tie your rushes
in their child days

pray at your wells

strong seas and broken waves
bore them off
from their green world to
this unimaginable land

here
other forces were at work
a saint—unseen—could be forgotten

I never heard you speak
or heard you spoken of
that dark threshold was never crossed
from you to me

my silent ancestors
how they kept their privacy

spiritual orphan
till I found you

Figure 3. *Holy Brighid Holding the World in Her Hands*. Maquette transferred to three 3 x 8-foot pieces of mahogany plywood to create a 9 x 8-foot mural that combines themes of the Divine Feminine with themes of world peace. Created for the Seventy-two Hours of Interfaith Peacemaking planned to mark the millennium. The mural has been hosted at the Interfaith Center at the Presidio in San Francisco, the NROOGD Brighid ritual in Berkeley, PantheaCon, and many other venues. It often graces the front yard of the artist's home. Painting by Rev. Rowan Fairgrove EPs.

A Transmission from the Goddess

Kelley Eileen Ingols

I am Brigid—Breet—who is within each of you. I hold the eternal flame within your sacred self. This fire never dies out. The flame within your womb space sparks through the darkness with creativity and inspiration. It rises up into your heart so that what is being fueled is nurtured with love. The flame rises into your throat so that you can express through your words what you desire to put out into the world. The flame is held in your head full of the wisdom and knowledge that is always within you.

I stand at the thresholds—the in-between places that honor the courage within to be brave, strong, confident to forge your way through the obstacles and barriers. Once you proceed and cross over, there is no going back, and your life will take you on a new journey and path if you are willing and ready.

I am here and ready to midwife you through what is ready to be born. Are you ready? The fire within has helped grow those seeds that are here at this time ready to emerge. Let them out. They are ready for this time.

I carry a sword along with a shield to be on the battlefield. I am not thirsty for blood and revenge. I am thirsty for truth and justice. I will help you with your battles and the battles that we stand for and with. Our time is calling for you and us to enter these battles with a new spark to fuel the flames through visions to heal by being sovereign.

I am here to help us smithcraft and forge our weapons that will empower us to choose our battles and be the voices of the people, the children, the animals, the plants, and this planet.

Help me by opening and spreading my cloak, which will protect and preserve our sacred lands.

There are many stories and myths about me. I crossed through the times when men and women once worshipped the rhythms of nature. I survived by being made a saint, and I am now being seen again in many different ways. Change, dear sister and brother. For we can change the ways that we perceive these times and our realities. Morph into what pulls and tugs at your heartstrings. We can become anyone and everything that calls our souls out of the darkness and into the light. Never forget the darkness, because that is when we rest, dream, and get recharged.

Let us heal together, heal ourselves, heal each other, and heal our lovely earth. We are no longer alone and stand stronger united.

I am awakening you once again as we emerge from our hibernation and come back into the light. Celebrate this time and spend time outside witnessing all that is rising and emerging within and without.

So it is. Blessed Imbolc.

Brigid's Return

Gera Clark

Over the shores I stood watching
as the sun burst forth a new day
though the waves were crashing
my mind poured into the beams of orange
lighting up the cliffs from their ashen array of greys
transmuting the solid craggy cut edges
to a soft haze upon which
I floated in clouds onto the green grasses
shamrocks sprouting beneath my feet
to feed the lambs born that day
As I set foot upon a place I would never leave
Gods and goddesses behold the healing
ancient energy of a land born before my time
Bless us all this day and may we walk the hills
and glens in peace and sleep well under the
the rain on our roofs while the distant shepherd
plays his song to his flock and the dogs lie down
to dream
Éire land
to dream
to rise again at dawn

Figure 4. Francis J. "Frank" McCabe, head of F Company, 1st Battalion, Dublin Brigade, Irish Volunteers. Frank joined the Volunteers in 1913. In this photo he is wearing the first official uniform of the Republic of Ireland, even though it was still under British rule when the Rising took place in 1916. Note the shamrocks on the buttons. "We serve neither King nor Kaiser but Ireland!" was their call. Photo from the private collection of Gera Clark, Francis McCabe's granddaughter.

Brigid of the Stars

Maria Jones

Since the beginning of time, priestesses have watched the starlit skies for signs and omens. Through their deep understanding of the cosmos, they prophesied the turning of the ages as they witnessed the shifting of one great cycle into another. They lived through times very similar to the one we find ourselves moving through now as we collectively journey into the Age of Aquarius.

In Goddess Astrology, the great goddess Brigid has a special connection with the sign of Aquarius. Her festival of Imbolc is celebrated during Aquarius season each year as the star fire of her inspiration begins to awaken within us once more after the long, cold winter months.

Aquarius is the sign that reminds us of our celestial origins. Like Brigid herself, Aquarius teaches us that we are all one with each other, the earth, and the cosmos. She teaches that we are each here to share our unique gifts and visions in service to the evolution of the whole.

What Sign Are You?

If you are not already familiar with your zodiac sign and your unique natal chart, you can obtain it by searching online for "free natal chart." You will need your date of birth, place of birth, and the time you were born for the most accurate interpretation. Once your chart is created, look first to your Sun's placement, then to the Moon and Ascendant (Rising) placements, for the most prominent manifestations of Brigid's energy in your celestial wheel. Be sure to look to other planetary placements and aspects as well for a fuller understanding of Brigid in your chart.

THE GODDESS IN THE SUN SIGNS

Through Brigid's gift of astrology, we are able to uncover how we may best be of service to her, and to humanity itself, as we move through these times of change. Within the twelve archetypes, or houses, of the zodiac, we see the many faces of Brigid reflected back at us. By understanding our own natal charts, we reveal the ways Brigid seeks to express herself through us, so that we may bring her healing wisdom out into the world.

First House–Aries

As an Aries, you are a Priestess of the Flaming Forge. Within your fire, weapons of personal power and righteousness are birthed. Your red-hot intensity burns away the past and reveals the gold of the soul that lies in the heart of every being. In your heat, your destiny is formed.

As the warrioress of Brigid's Cosmic Wheel, you are the initiator of the new. You are the spark of inspiration that illuminates the pathway forward, the beginning of all things. You are she who empowers all people to follow their hearts' passion. It is you who wields her blazing sword of truth, cutting away inauthenticity and fear. You are the slayer of the demons of procrastination and the protectress of the innocent.

If you have planets in the First House and/or have strong planetary aspects to Mars, you will also feel the influence of Brigid's Aries energy.

Second House–Taurus

As a Taurus, you are a Priestess of the Beauty Way. You are the energy of Brigid the Great Cow Mother. You are her stream of sustenance flowing from the Milky Way, nourishing us spiritually and emotionally.

Dependable and solid, you are the nurturer, she who blesses her people with a never-ending supply of abundance. You remind us of the fertile, life-giving qualities of Brigid, she who teaches us that we are all worthy and deserving of living a bountiful life filled with beauty. You are Brigid of the Flowers, radiant with the joy of life. You show us how to be the embodiment of her love, to accept the gifts and pleasures she offers to us.

If you have planets in the Second House and/or have strong planetary aspects to Venus, you will also feel the influence of Brigid's Taurus energy.

Third House–Gemini

As a Gemini, you are a Priestess of Word Weaving. You are Brigid's sacred scribe. You are her poetess and her voice. You are a vessel of her genius, here to share wisdom and expanded viewpoints that help us see with fresh eyes.

You teach us to sound our soul note, to speak our truth and share her messages with the world. You are her wordsmith, her bard who sings the song of her love out into the world. You are the speaker of her words of comfort, courage, and illumination. You show others how to liberate their throat chakras and rewrite their personal mythology into a story of healing and empowerment.

If you have planets in the Third House and/or have strong planetary aspects to Mercury, you will also feel the influence of Brigid's Gemini energy.

Fourth House–Cancer

As a Cancer, you are a Priestess of Home and Hearth. You are Brigid's keeper of the home fire. You are the guardian of the family and lineage, the tender of the wellspring of love that is at the center of all things. You are the creator of safe space and the teacher of vulnerability.

You are the soft embrace of Brigid as Great Mother, she who heals and cares for our inner child and all the children of the world. You are the chalice of healing that soothes and cleanses the deepest wounds of the soul, the memory of resting in her great womb floating in her amniotic fluid of unconditional love.

If you have planets in the Fourth House and/or have strong planetary aspects to the Moon, you will also feel the influence of Brigid's Cancer energy.

Fifth House—Leo

As a Leo, you are a Priestess of the Solar Fire. You are here to shine Brigid's flame of creativity and warmth into the world. You are her birthing creatrix, inspiring others with your unique gifts and talents.

You show us how to radiate her light unapologetically and fiercely as we walk her pathway of service. You remind us to have the courage to follow our hearts and bravely stand up and be seen. You teach us the importance of self-love and sovereignty as we dance our desires into being. You are the golden goddess claiming the divine nectar of life through the embodiment of your own power.

If you have planets in the Fifth House and/or have strong planetary aspects to the Sun, you will also feel the influence of Brigid's Leo energy.

Sixth House—Virgo

As a Virgo, you are a Priestess of the Devotional Flame. You are the keeper of her flame. Like the Brigidine nuns who, to this day, keep Brigid's altar flame alight at Kildare, you guide us in the sacred arts of discipline and dedication upon the spiritual pathway.

You teach the powers of humility and simplicity, desiring only to serve and heal in her name. Intuitively you understand the powers of the herbs, minerals, and elements needed to realign the body and soul. You remind us that the mundane is sacred, that the small moments and details are what make life truly magical. You are the tender of the temple, the creator of ritual and ceremony.

If you have planets in the Sixth House and/or have strong planetary aspects to Mercury, you also will feel the influence of Brigid's Virgo energy.

Seventh House—Libra

As a Libra, you are a Priestess of Justice and Balance. You are Brigid's bringer of balance and her emissary of justice, focused on what is fair and true.

Like Brigid marrying Bres to unite the warring tribes, you teach us the power of conflict resolution and understanding of karmic law, bringing peace and harmony to troubled times. You are Brigid as the Bride, offering the medicine of healing through relationship. You gift us the teaching of soft power, of living from the heart's truth. You know that there is a time for compromise and a time to take a stand.

If you have planets in the Seventh House and/or have strong planetary aspect to Venus, you will also feel the influence of Brigid's Libra energy.

Eighth House–Scorpio

As a Scorpio, you are a Priestess of the Cauldron of Alchemy. You are Brigid's black fire of transformation. Like her serpent, you teach us how to shed our old skin and rebirth ourselves.

You are her prophetess, her sybil, seeing beyond the veil and whispering visions of the ancestors. You teach us the secrets of the alchemical fires of the forge, transmuting the pain of trauma into spiritual illumination. You are Brigid who knows the depths of grief, keening for her lost son. You are the keeper of her shadow mysteries. You are she who knows that the darkest hour comes before the dawn.

If you have planets in the Eighth House and/or have strong planetary aspects to Pluto, you will also feel the influence of Brigid's Scorpio energy.

Ninth House–Sagittarius

As a Sagittarius, you are a Priestess of the Fiery Arrow. You are Brigid's "breo-saighead," her fiery arrow. Born under the sign of the Cosmic Archeress, you are her Huntress of Wisdom, reconnecting us to our inner wild and wise woman!

Always seeking truth, you are her fire of knowledge, her teacher. Like the old wizard Merlin's vision of Brigid, you see to the furthest edges of the cosmos, bringing understanding of the divine plan and taking us beyond our small human perceptions. You are her shepherdess, guiding others toward deeper spiritual realizations. You are her lantern in the dark, bringing hope, faith, and clarity during times of uncertainty.

If you have planets in the Ninth House and/or have strong planetary aspects to Jupiter, you will also feel the influence of Brigid's Sagittarius energy.

Tenth House–Capricorn

As a Capricorn, you are a Priestess of Ancestral Wisdom. You manifest the energy of Brigid of the Ancestors. You are a priestess of her ancient mysteries, from the times before time. You are the geomancer, the one who speaks with the spirits of the standing stones.

You are her keeper of ancestral lineage, the wisdom in our bones that speaks to us the secrets of those who walked this pathway long before us. You bring us the gifts of patience, integrity, and longevity. In old Celtic folklore, it is said that, if you repeat the genealogy of Brigid, you will always be watched over. You are the one who offers up that sacred prayer, the one who protects and provides. You are the wizened grandmother who asks us what legacy we wish to leave behind for future generations.

If you have planets in the Tenth House and/or have strong planetary aspects to Saturn, you will also feel the influence of Brigid's Capricorn energy.

Eleventh House–Aquarius

As an Aquarius, you are a Priestess of Star Fire. You are the keeper of Brigid's heavenly flame. Born at the time of Imbolc, you bring her gifts of awakening and inspiration. Carrying the cup of the Water Bearer, you are her holy well maiden, pouring her crystalline waters of purification upon us all.

You bring her gifts of soul liberation and cosmic vision, blessing us with the touch of the muse that ignites the creativity of the soul. As Brigid herself evolved from venerated figure to goddess to exalted saint at the end of the last great age, you teach us how to adapt to the new. You give us fresh perspectives and clear eyes through which to look at life. You are the guide of the dawning Aquarian Era, bringing gifts of community, connection, and expansion.

If you have planets in the Eleventh House and/or strong planetary aspects to Uranus, you will also feel the influence of Brigid's Aquarius energy.

Twelfth House–Pisces

As a Pisces, you are a Priestess of Soul Surrender. You are Brigid's soul healer. Like her sacred swan, you travel the astral currents and slip between worlds. You stand with ease in the liminal spaces. You are her snow-white wings, enveloping us in her benediction and mercy.

You are the carrier of her healing mantle, she who restores innocence and purity, who soothes all wounds with her balm of compassion. You teach us the art of surrender, the letting go of control that comes when we recognize that she is always there, walking beside us. You are the unconditional love of Brigid expressed through art, poetry, and music. You teach us how to see with eyes of divinity, remembering that we are all one with each other and with her.

If you have planets in the Twelfth House and/or strong planetary aspects to Neptune, you will also feel the influence of Brigid's Pisces energy.

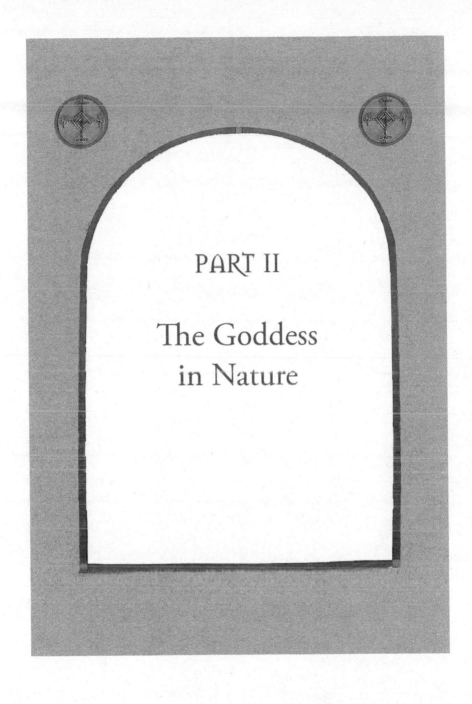

PART II

The Goddess
in Nature

Brighid of the Dandelion

Jenne Micale

You are in the dandelion, the gold
of the summer your bright eye, its edged lace
your mantle winter white in the grass, each

sailing on the wind to root in new ground.
After frost they still reached out to bloom, burning
in dim Samhaintide up until the snow

where under that blank mantle they abide
until the first fetching thaw. Roots reach deep
and ensure their return, the same as thought,

as a smoored flame slumbering in heaps of
snowy ash until the wind of a word
stirs it, a willing hand readies a twig

and so brings back day's flame, the saving heat.
You cannot be eradicated, fire-eye
and pale foot, the heat of thought melting the ice.

The Swarm

Laura Louella

It is spring and there is a shift in the hive. It is buzzing with new activity. There is an energetic difference. The bees are preparing for something. They have an innate knowing that a transition is coming. The colony trusts their intuition; they know how to deal with this time of change.

The hive is healthy and thriving. There are so many bees that it's beginning to feel crowded. The queen has begun to release less pheromone. She knows it's time to abdicate her throne. The worker bees are feeding the queen less food in order to help her lose a little weight so that she can fly. The workers are also moving the queen about the hive to prevent her from laying too many eggs. The colony is working together for the good of the whole. The worker bees begin to eat more, gorging themselves on honey, getting ready for the work ahead. It is amazing that they can eat so much and still fly!

The colony's bees are prodding the old queen to fly with them. Suddenly there is a huge, moving, black, swirl of bees. This intricate dance is being performed by the honeybees who know innately that it's time to go. At least half of the bees have left the nest. As they fly, the old queen chooses a structure and lands there; the workers immediately surround her. They keep her safe and cool. While most of the bees tend their queen, a few scouts leave to find the perfect place for a new hive. The scouts sometimes locate the perfect place in a few hours; sometimes it may take a few days to find a suitable location. This large cluster of bees may draw a lot of attention if they land in a tree or on someone's mailbox. But, because the swarm does not have a brood or food stores to defend, they are docile and can be observed safely.

The worker bees in the old hive are raising a new queen, feeding the chosen larva large quantities of royal jelly. When the virgin queen emerges, she remains in the hive for about one week to let the remaining worker bees become accustomed to her. She will then take her maiden flight to mate with the drones, a process that could last up to three days. This one mating cycle will provide her with enough sperm to fertilize eggs for the next two to five years. When she returns to the hive, her worker bees will attend to her needs. The queen relies heavily on her worker bees to care for her so that she can do her job. She will be the mother of all of the bees in the hive. She lays the eggs that will become female worker bees and male drones, and one that will someday become the next virgin queen. Much like our resilient mothers, the queen works each day to ensure there are eggs in each cell of the hive. The maternal line continues unbroken. From mother to daughter, for generations, this will take place.

Meanwhile, the scouts return to where the old queen is waiting and begin to perform a complex dance, called the waggle dance. This dance is usually done to tell other honeybees where the pollen can be gathered, but, in this instance, the bees know that the scouts are conveying that they have found a place to create a new hive. These scouts sometimes have to encourage the bees to follow them. Finally, they lead the old queen to the new location and she settles in. Workers start building the honeycomb and the queen begins to lay her eggs in the empty cells. The workers resume their duties raising brood and gathering and storing food. There is ample time to build the colony's numbers and food stores before the cold winter returns.

Now, where there was one hive, there are two; instead of one queen, there are two. With more honeybees to pollinate our flowers and food, the whole ecosystem is stronger.

The swarm feels very much like my life at present. I have had to gather my mother and all of her possessions and move her to a place of her choosing. She is trusting me to do the work, just as the queen trusts her worker bees to do the work that creates a new hive for her. While this work is new, challenging, and life-changing, I have come to realize the parallels that exist between the hive and society.

As I go through the process and compare the two, I see the similarities of daughters caring for their mothers. The worker bees honor the queen, yet some of modern society doesn't appreciate the natural process. Instead, it sees this time of life as an imposition and a burden. While I also had feelings of being overwhelmed by this process, studying the bees gave me a new appreciation and I am humbled that I have the ability to care for my mom. I have been moved to appreciate this part of the natural world. Mom is now the old queen and I am both a worker bee and the new queen. Making her comfortable and keeping her safe are one job. Another is to create a new life where the old one was.

As I am preparing for the winter of my mother's life, I am reminded that, for generations, this has gone on in the lives of my ancestors. Caring for the elderly and creating a new way of being are in my DNA. It is who my family is. We care for each other. This has been a lived example for as long as I can remember, and in the stories I was told of times before I was here. We sacrifice; we move; we change; we honor in order to keep the old queen safe and comfortable as she enters this phase of life. This is my example of how to care for community, how to think about the greater good. In doing so, old wounds can be healed and I am showing the next generation how to care for their queen.

I wonder, when the bees swarm, if they are frightened by the change. Are they apprehensive? Do they inherently trust? Is it in their knowing that this is the way of the world? Have they known for all time that this is how community functions? The bees truly are our teachers. I am looking more and more to the hive, watching how they spend their lives caring for the good of the colony.

I see the goddess Brigid here. She calls us, leads us, and inspires us to do the work that our communities need. She is the spark of spring that calls forth the warmth to thaw our land. Brigid calls the magic of the fertile earth to new life with her bright light. Flowers bloom and bees return.

When the time is right, Brigid is the fire that produces the smoke to calm the bees so that swarms can be gathered and re-hived. Her smoke also allows us to gather the golden elixir from the hive. She is the shining example of care for all living things, showing us that we are intimately connected and all the same.

The Furor of the River

Michael Routery

I remember how
I rode behind the Lady
on her sturdy and swift steed
through the drizzle and the shimmer
always a promise of rainbow
and the roar of sea receding
but came we near that great
onslaught of river
the furor of its course
of inspiration,
such eddies and swirls
in its current.
It fills with wisdom
as it issues from the sacred well
where the hazel trees grow.
I was fertile with the dark speech
She informed and took me back
to the cliff where large birds sang
and I fell back asleep and
dreamed of being torn by sharp beaks,
my organs rearranged to make more space
for the poems that baked within.

Brighid as a Water Goddess

Annwyn Avalon

Brighid, goddess of wisdom, poetry, and healing, is best known for her connection to fire and the sacred flame. However, it was in her guise as a goddess of water that I met her for the first time. Brighid may be connected with the hearth, fire, wisdom, and poetry, but because of her many sacred wells, she is also considered a water goddess. Sacred springs and holy wells throughout Ireland, Scotland, Wales, and England bear her name, and she is honored and worshipped at numerous watery sites throughout the Celtic lands. The river Breint, in Anglesey, Wales, is named for her.

Folk magic practices preserved not only Brighid's legend, but the way she once was honored by our ancestors. Some of these practices include visiting her sacred wells, decorating them on sacred or holy days, and circumambulation. Clooties once were, and still are, placed in trees by those who seek her wise and healing waters.

Clooties (or clouties) are strips of fabric torn from clothing and used in healing rituals connected to sacred wells. Traditionally, the fabric was torn from the clothing of the person seeking healing, then dipped in water from a sacred well while uttering incantations and prayers, and hung in a nearby sacred tree. Through the process of magical transfer and petitioning Brighid for healing, wisdom, and blessings, the illness left the body as the strip of fabric disintegrated. Today, sacred springs and holy wells are decorated with these clooties. Although now they are often referred to as prayer ribbons, they certainly flow back to ancestral clootie practices. To recreate these rituals today, we must take the environment into account and adjust our rituals to preserve the sacred natural places where her magical waters flow forth. Synthetic fabrics, for instance, are not biodegradable, and so should be avoided.

I met Brighid during one of my visits to England—a trip to visit family. But a small detour to Somerset and to the magical town of Glastonbury changed my life forever. It was there that I met the goddess in a dark watery candlelit temple. My heart skipped a beat. She took my breath away. I remember it as if it were yesterday.

I entered her temple with reverence, not knowing what I would find beyond those darkened doors. I walked barefoot upon a cold stone floor saturated with water. As I wound through the temple exploring the mysterious nature of this sacred place, I came upon Brighid, larger than life, at the back of a hazel-twig cavern covered in charms, votive offerings, and clooties.

There she stood, clothed in a dark-blue hooded robe that resembled a gentle waterfall cascading over a cliff, her mysterious face illuminated by the sacred flame. It felt as if she were extending her arms toward my astonished self, as if she were passing the flame to me. Fire has always been a mystery to me, but now I wondered if this water goddess could teach me the power and magic of fire in a way that I had never understood before.

Today, for me, Brighid is a water goddess and I can connect, through her, with the element of fire. Fire has always been a difficult element for me. While I love candle magic and it has always been central to my practice, an intimate understanding of fire eluded me for a long time. It was, in fact, Brighid's watery influence that led me to a deeper understanding of fire and the balance that exists between these two elements. I now honor her as a goddess of both water and fire by combining these elements on her altar. I also honor Brighid at her altar by decorating it with icons and statues of the goddess, three- and four-armed Brighid's Crosses, a silver dish for incense, and, most important, a representation of her sacred well. This is, in fact, the focal point of her altar where I scry and work watery healing magic or commune with her.

You can create your own sacred well to place on Brighid's altar. Begin by choosing a surface and finding the right location. Cover the surface that will become your altar with a cloth of your choice. I recommend blue or green to connect with her water aspect. Blue can represent water, while green can represent earth, the vessel that holds the sacred waters. Use your intuition and listen to her guidance.

Next, choose a sacred vessel. This can be metal, glass, or ceramic, depending on how you intend to use it. Metal bowls are beautiful, but do not always fare well long term. Glass bowls can also work well, but if you decide to use a candle as described below, it may break from the heat. I prefer ceramic bowls, because I like their earthy feel, and because they are strong and can hold water over a long period of time.

Place the bowl in the center of your altar or in an area on your altar that has several inches all around. You can decorate around the bowl as you would a sacred well for different sabbats, sacred days, or rituals. Use natural items like leaves and twigs, flowers, and crystals. Alternatively, you can place a tray in the center of the altar and decorate it with moss, flowers, and other greenery, then place the vessel that represents the sacred well in the center. This gives it a natural look and resembles old well-dressing customs.

Once your sacred well is set, you must choose your water. Water from one of Brighid's many sacred wells is ideal, of course. But if this is not available to you, work with spring, river, or snow water. These other waters can be used for specific purposes. Snow or ice water is appropriate for her sacred sabbat, Imbolc. Dew can also be used, although it requires quite a bit of work to collect enough of it to fill a sacred vessel. You can add a few drops to spring water around Beltane. Floral waters, especially those sacred to Brighid and those that have fire and solar correspondences, can be used as offerings, while summer water is perfect for her altar during the warmer months.

Building a sacred well on your altar is a great way to connect with Brighid through her water aspect. However, you can also work with her sacred flame *within* this sacred well. In this case, you will need a strong ceramic bowl that can stand up to heat. Place your candle in the center of the dry bowl using wax adhesive, melting and manipulating the wax to stick the candle to the bottom of the bowl. Then pour your sacred water into the vessel, saying:

> Water spiral from below
> Rise up and help me grow.

Light the candle and say:

> Ignite the sacred fire,
> Brighid my heart's desire.

Place both hands gently around the bowl and say:

Brighid of the sacred flame
I call thee forth by holy name.

Brighid of the waters deep
Reveal the visions I do seek.

Finish with your own words, asking for Brighid's blessings and any messages she may bring. You can now scry the water, the flame, or both.

Figure 5. Brigid and the King's Wolf. Inspired by the legend of Brigid and the King's Wolf, Val Damon and her mother, Jean Hendon, collaborated to create a sort of rosary that combines Jean's paintings and Val's silverwork. Using a technique called *stucco Veneziano,* a technique used in the Sistine Chapel, Val formed sterling silver into bezels and filled them with a special type of concrete made with marble dust, which Jean then painted with oil paint and gilded with gold leaf. Natural serpentine stones adorn the pendant as a tribute to the Serpents of Imbolc. The cut of the stones hearkens back to Brigid's earliest incarnations; chip-stone necklaces have been used to form shamanic altars since ancient times. What began as a rosary became a type of personal altar with Brigid's white wolf as the focal point. Photo by Paul Lindholm.

Birch Wheel

Donna Gerrard

If I were a tree, I would be a silver birch,
stepping lightly out of dainty earth shoes,
dancing wind-whisked to a new home.
A swish-skirted gipsy wearing black and silver bangles.

If I were a tree, I would be a silver birch,
a fertile flirtatious maiden,
my slender arms aching to cradle babies, tickling the reticent sky
    until
he stirs and responds to my rustling giggle.

If I were a tree, I would be a silver birch,
a memory of glacier glistening in my curling elven armor,
my axe-handle trunk cleaving green spring wounds
that run with the purifying snowmelt in my veins.

If I were a tree, I would be a silver birch,
my trunk the pale, lined finger of a sprightly crone
pressed to the whispering lips of the wind,
to besom-sweep her memory from men.

Brigid of the Ozarks

Tara Anura

Brigid is everywhere in the Missouri Ozarks. She's in the bluegrass fiddle music whose rhythms and lyrics changed as Scottish and Irish immigrants adapted to new lands while crossing Appalachia and the Great Smokies, eventually settling in the Ozarks. Along the way, it collected the rhythms of Africa and instruments like the banjo and mouth harp. It is jubilant music that is also touched with sorrow and echoes of the past. Once, standing on a mountainside, I heard that music echoing across the hills from a music festival in the river valley several miles away. But I couldn't hear Brigid in the music at that time. I knew her rather in the springs that burst forth from the earth's belly to fill the creeks and rivers with tens of thousands of gallons of water daily. These were the holy waters in which my maternal grandpa baptized me.

Unlike the mighty Mississippi, most of Missouri's rivers are clear and shallow. Decades later, I can still remember how the water's music went from high tones to deep as Grandpa lowered me back and my ears filled with icy liquid. I can see the tiny minnow that swam by amid bits of stringy plants, quickly disappearing in the river muck stirred up by our bare feet. I can hear gravel clacking, displaced by our feet and tossed by the current.

When you are pulled up from an icy river that has been winding for miles underground in caves, your body inhales hard without consulting you. I imagine it's how a newborn baby feels taking its first frigid breath after being in a warm womb for so long. There is an instant of separation in which you don't control your muscles or lungs. You shake and you aren't sure if it's hypothermia, Jesus, the Holy Spirit, or all three. That's why Ozark church and tent revivals happen mostly in the summer. You don't get as many converts if you have to crack river ice to baptize them.

My parents baptized me right away as an infant, but my subsequent preteen baptism was for me. My mother wasn't happy when I told her that my first baptism had been for the family; I couldn't remember it, after all. She made sure that I knew she had done it to save my soul from hell. She got angry when I accused her of lying, saying that we had to wear frilly church dresses for other people, not for God. I wanted something more than a story about how someone sprinkled water on my head in a church. All I had seen of my baptism was the professional sepia-tone photograph my mother treasured: "Isn't the photo of you in that white dress and cap the most precious thing?"

But I didn't want a religious experience performed for others and unremembered by me. I wanted to be cleansed and embraced by nature. From the age of five, I had experienced sexual, verbal, physical, and emotional abuse. I thought that, if I had a second baptism, God and nature would wash away all of my inner turmoil, my self-loathing, my pain, and maybe even the memories. Maybe my baptism would bring the Holy Spirit down on my family and make them more loving. So, at my second baptism, I kept my eyes open. But I still didn't see the goddess who was there.

As a child in the late 1980s, the only name I knew for the Divine Feminine was Mary. Mary, I was taught, was holy because she was the vessel used by the Holy Ghost to conceive Jesus. I'd learned that babies came from a man and a woman—a sperm and an egg—and my strict mother, a pastor's wife, was shocked when I asked how God put the sperm into Mary. She said it was a miracle; the Holy Spirit came down to her, and that's what mattered. I ran around the house with my arms akimbo, wailing that I was the Holy Ghost until my mother yelled: "That is enough; don't mock God!" Mother usually spoke very proper English until she was mad, then God became Gawd and you knew you were about to be put in the corner. "You watch your mouth!" she'd warn. "'Darn' is the same as cussing! Gawd knows what you mean!"

My family is a melting pot of many places and people, just like many Americans. My parents were Methodist, and my grandpa a Baptist minister. His father was descended from a long line of German Lutheran rebels who probably broke away from the Catholic Church when Martin Luther did. Many German families fled the tiny kingdoms run by tyrant princes and bishops and came to Pennsylvania in the 1700s and 1800s, then settled in northern Missouri. It's challenging to find a sense of inherited sacredness, religious roots, and customs beyond American capitalistic pop culture and Christianity. I struggled with that, and still do.

In my own American crazy-quilt family, a thread starting with Grandpa's mother weaves from the Missouri Ozarks, back to the Eastern Seaboard, and across the Atlantic to the Caudles, a family that lived in a region that straddles the border between Scotland and England. Around 1827, the Caudles immigrated to America. Elizabeth Verner Boyd Caudle, my great-great-great-grandmother, had a daughter named Sarah, who in turn had a daughter named Sarah Jane. Sarah Jane married into the German immigrant farming community of Yount, Missouri. She had five children, one of whom was my grandpa. Other Scottish and Scots-Irish bloodlines, like the Boyds, stitch the family quilt together.

My family told me that I was the spitting image of Sarah Jane, my great-grandmother, who was born in 1891. My mom, sisters, and I often sat with Grandma Lois looking through shoeboxes and albums full of old photos. When Mom found a picture of Sarah Jane, her eyes widened and she grinned and said: "Here's Sarah Jane. Doesn't Tara look just like her?" I was maybe nine when I first held her picture. It was uncanny to see an older version of myself sitting with a serious face—plump and soft, yet somehow hardened by life—surrounded by people I'd never met. The way time and genetics swirled from my flesh-and-blood hand to the fragile photograph of someone who wasn't me, but someone whom I would be like someday, made my head spin. I closed my eyes for a moment and handed the picture back quickly. Over the years, I've often touched that photo and seemed to hear her saying my name, although we never met. Sarah Jane died when my mom was still a young girl.

My family told me that Sarah Jane had been a midwife and a healer when doctors were rare in the Ozarks. She traveled alone to the homes of people who were ill. Sometimes entire families were sick. Sarah Jane went into the barn and changed into different clothes before going in to care for them. She washed her hands constantly with hot water and soap. Nursing a patient or family back to health often took days of mixing remedies and feeding them. Once a patient either died or was cured, she went into the smokehouse (if it was big enough) or behind the barn for modesty, where she stripped down, burned the clothes she was wearing, washed up, and put on other clothes before going home. She did this to protect her children.

Sarah Jane was a healer, a midwife, and a flame-keeper. And she raised cows. All these activities fall under Brigid's matronage as a saint, according to folklore and the Catholic Church. Sarah Jane raised her children and birthed many others in the small community. Premature infants were placed close to a hearth or woodstove with a carefully banked fire. She taught the parents how to tend this primitive incubator. I don't know if she honored or worshipped Brigid in some way. Did she petition the Divine Feminine for aid when wiping someone's brow or birthing babies? Saints' days were struck from the liturgical calendar in many faiths. Did members of the Mt. Zion Lutheran Church in Yount talk about Saint Brigid?

Every summer, all of us cousins were sent to my grandparents for three glorious months away from screaming, belts, and slaps. Grandma and Grandpa didn't argue nearly as much as my parents did, so it was a glorious reprieve out in nature, running along the deer trails, playing in the creek, and fishing in the pond. Grandpa was an expert fire-keeper. He could do controlled burns on his land, start a fire in his fireplace at home, and light the woodstove in the hunting cabin he had built. My favorite time was getting up before my loud cousins did, and sitting and watching Grandpa build a fire at dawn. Staring into a fire and listening to the wood crackle relaxed me.

As a teenager, I carried a lighter in my pocket and often lit it just to stare into the flame. "Light a candle, stare into the flame," a voice urged me in a whisper. Sometimes it was Sarah Jane, sometimes another divine voice. "Come into the flame." When I was three and couldn't use matches, I begged my mom to light candles so I could watch them dance and feel their comfort. As a teen, I lit candles and sat and meditated, envisioning the flame merging with my heart and then separating. Sometimes I swayed gently, mimicking the flame's dance. A being of power and unconditional love lived in the flame. I kept my time with her secret so my family wouldn't think I was a crazy sinner.

I joined the Girl Scouts to build campfires and sit around them. I became a camp counselor so I could continue to do so as I got older. Decades later, as my twenty-year marriage was falling apart, I got a call from a high school friend. We had been Girl Scouts and camp counselors together. She invited me to an overnight camp reunion close to my summer birthday.

I know now that that overnight reunion was a test run for living on my own. Could I leave my abusive partner for a night and find myself? We had married when I was twenty and he was eighteen. We had grown up together, lived as lovers and best friends, and then, when I began to demand respect, we became worst enemies. Could I escape the gaslighting and ridicule, the trauma disguised as love? Could I escape suicidal ideation and my attempts to end my life?

I drove over the hills and through the valleys, back to the place where I had stood on the side of the mountain and heard bluegrass music echoing for miles. My body remembered, and it rang and vibrated in a way I hadn't felt before. The promise of freedom and rediscovery ignited in my heart and crackled across my skin.

Girl Scouts at camp don't just throw wood into a pit, spray it with fuel, and light it. No. It's a sacred rite. A flame-tender organizes the gathering of the kindling and logs and has the honor of sparking the flame that will warm bodies and souls. She keeps the fire burning until the last song fades and women start to wander back to their cots. Women gathered away from the male gaze, away from male aggression, away from male assumptions. Free women. Their laughter, tears, and songs connect the sunset's flame to the fire and, later, the fire to the stars. By the lake, sitting around the fire in quiet contemplation, we listened to the frogs and watched an eagle circle above us. We all stared silently into the fire and listened. That's when Brigid told me this was a new beginning.

I returned home a different woman, and my husband knew it. Eventually, he began sleeping on the couch. Finally, I lit my torch and told him to leave. After he left, I often crawled into bed and sobbed myself to sleep. Days blurred into nights. Nights became weeks. I reached out to priestesses I knew. They all promised the crying would end.

My subsequent baptism was by both fire and water.

I threw copies of my psychiatric records and the workplace sexual harassment case I had filed into a box, and I drove to the river. I collected kindling and wood, and built a fire right there on the concrete boat launch. I prayed no one would drive up. This place was mine. My life was mine, and I chose to set it on fire. I grabbed a big poking stick and tossed those papers into the flames a few at a time. In went the documents that said there wasn't enough evidence of sexual harassment. Case closed. In went the reports from all the times I had been hospitalized because baptism and prayers couldn't end my pain. Ended. In went the papers that told of how I tried to end my life to end the pain. Gone. I watched the pages turn red at the edges then blacken, and knew that I was finally strong enough to get a toxic family and spouse out of my life.

As I added the last handful of paper, the wind moved through the forest and whipped my hair about my face. I used the stick to push the flaming pile into the water. The current caught it and turned my past devastations into floating mini-pyres that moved swiftly downstream. There was music in the river, music in the wind, music in the trees, and birdsong all around. I saw Brigid and Oshun standing on the river—Brigid of my Scottish and Irish ancestors and Oshun of the African people brought to the Ozarks to mine iron ore and smelt it into the bars used by well-paid white blacksmiths. I waded out after the floating flames until I was waist-deep in the icy water. I splashed and flung water to put out the fire of my anger and torment.

The water rose high into the air and sprinkled down on my head. I speared the papers and pushed them, steaming and sizzling, to the bottom of the shallow river. If they popped up, I tore the sodden pages and submerged them again. I wanted no one to see my personal pain and discover my name. And then I had a thought. I would legally change my name. I would drop the name chosen by men and pick the last name I wanted. Waist-deep in that river, smelling like fish and smoke, I gave a warrior cry and threw the stick like a spear. I raised my hands, looked at the sky, and laughed.

I no longer wait for one miraculous moment or one ritual to heal me. Every day is an opportunity to be grateful for life. Being fully present in this body is the most healing gift of all. Thank you, Brigid of the Ozarks—bright, comforting voice in the flame and water.

Why Not?

Sister Karol Jackowski

In tending Brigid's flame
(never extinguished),
I bet you hear what I hear
when Brigid speaks
in flames that consume us—
"Why not become fire?"

In tending Brigid's flame,
she tends ours
(never extinguished).
She hears what we hear
in flames that consume us—
the unspeakable,
the unbearable,
the incomprehensible.
I bet you hear what I hear
when Brigid whispers
in every consuming flame—
"Why not become fire?"

In tending Brigid's flame
(never extinguished),
as she tends soul-fires too,
something happens
without notice.
Something Happens.
Abracadabra.

In tending Brigid's flame
(never extinguished),

I pray you hear what I hear
in all Brigid's tending—
"What consumes you
makes you fire
with evermore power
to enlighten."

In tending Brigid's flame
(never extinguished),
she tends ours.
Never taking eyes off the flame,
we become fire.
"Why not?"

Figure 6. Brigid's Fire. This pen-and-ink, mixed-media drawing honors the many aspects and arts of Brigid, especially her ability to help clear out the old, forge new growth, and aid in honing personal power. Drawing by Laura Tempest Zakroff.

Brigid of Kildare

Carole Murray

Brigid reigns over the feast of Imbolc, one of the four feasts of the traditional Celtic ceremonial cycle. On February 1st, she was said to be seen emerging in the form of a snake from the cave where she had spent the winter. Her presence evoked the beginning of spring and the birthing time of lambs.

Brigid's sacred shrine still exists in Kildare, Ireland. In ancient times, nineteen virgins tended an undying flame; on the twentieth day, Brigid tended the fire by herself. For many centuries, that flame remained doused. But in 1993, the Sisters of Brigid relit the flame and they keep it burning as a symbol of healing and peace. Her sacred well is still in use as a healing shrine as well. Her commitment to healing is reflected in the words of a prayer traditionally attributed to her:

> I would like the angels of Heaven to be among us. I would like an abundance of peace. I would like full vessels of charity. I would like rich treasures of mercy. I would like cheerfulness to preside over all . . . I would like the friends of Heaven to be gathered around us from all parts. I would like a great lake of beer for the King of Kings. I would like to be watching Heaven's family drinking it through all eternity.

Since Brigid is the patron of poets, I dedicate the following poem to her.

> Imbolc
> We meet in a circle facing a frozen stone.
> We are the color of snow.
> Only our eyes make bright flames in the dark.
> Winter is almost over.
> Just today, something green stirred in the clumsy ice.
> The fast has been endless.

Ribs protrude: strings of a harp with no playing.
We sing with empty mouths praising the gods
Who keep us safe from the roasting fires.
It is good sometimes to wait,
As if there were a plan.
To shrink down to the spirit—
A ghost whose vigil
Hunger cannot keep.

Steep Green Heights

Michael Routery

Steep green heights, I climbed, high above the pounding
surf, on this island like so many pearling the Otherworld seas
where spring and summer reign eternal
a path flanked with calyxes
of blood red, and royal purples, botanic swords raised.
One unfolded like an elephant's ear,
another changing color according to the hours—
I can smell your fragrance, hear your songs chanted
by birds the color of honey and apples.

Your challenges, your riddles clung like dew
sticking on glossy foliage, amid
howling voices of unseen spirits.
I reached a verdant tableland where I could see
the endless blues of the sea afar off,
and set up camp. I would build up my strength
to continue in succeeding days, your song
running in my blood, plucking my tongue,
Goddess of the poets I descried you in
fern-lavished woods, in the gauze of waterfalls
and felt the painful losses here, but your
goad and the strains of your harp push me on.
I strive for your glen, your glade, your bower.
O Brigid, I raise my voice in your praise—
may this composition of flowers, green, red,
and speckled please on these steep green heights of poetry.

Weaving Spring

Mael Brigde

Brigit's Crosses are woven from rushes and other materials in a variety of designs to secure her protection on *Oiche Fhéile Bhríde* (Saint Brigit's Eve). This festival, also called Imbolc, marks the first day of spring. A burden-rope was made from grasses, horsehair, or rushes, and secured to itself with a wooden eye. It was used, often by women, to carry great burdens of hay, corn, or bushes. This poem celebrates both the power of the goddess and the strength of the women devoted to her.

Creased—calloused
stained with age

your hands free
fresh-pulled rushes
from the burden-rope

lift these few
with which you shape
the sunwise cross

the sun's eye turns—mild in your fingers—
three arms—four—constellations of diamonds
woven on joined sticks

year follows year
the mud of marshes
embellishing
the soles of your feet

red bracken
replaced by green
she comes anew—the springtime—you weave her in

Figure 7. Brigid of the Oak. In this piece, the artist honors the three aspects of Brigid. The oak leaves represent her earliest form as a goddess of the land among the sacred oak trees. The rush cross represents her sainted form after the advent of Christianity in Ireland and the British Isles. These two aspects combined, radiating in a sun-wheel formation, represent her dual divinity as a solar goddess and a saint heralding the light of half of the year. It is the artist's sigil for the great goddess of earth and fire. Hand-pulled linocut print by Holly Devanna.

An Old Seed

Jennifer Sundeen

this morning
I rose with the Imbolc sun
a faint pink blush on the new Bride's cheeks
and despite the old Crone's wintry howl
the glowing sky was a maiden's promise
of warmth and light
and of springtime soon to come

I thought of possibility
and of last year's seed packages
twine-bound
buried in the recesses of the kitchen cupboard
some I never got around to opening
some with remnants of extra seeds
that for many reasons went unsown

shall I plant them this year
and see what takes hold?
or start fresh
call the seed company
place a new order
to guarantee a fruitful harvest come autumn?

a small bag of bean seeds
still sits on my kitchen counter
gifted from the garden of a departed friend
they are seven years old now
but I cannot yet bear to let them go

sometimes we hang on
far longer than we should

but sometimes
even an old seed
against all probability
despite all odds
suddenly feels a certain stirring

and with the fiery surge of new life again
she shoots her newfound leg-roots downward
then rises, strong and determined,
makes her way around sharp stones
through the dark cloak of heavy soil
forging ever upward

until one magical day
she bursts out into the light
into this great waiting world
graced now with time-earned courage, with wisdom
ready at long last to share
her most perfect and fullest bloom

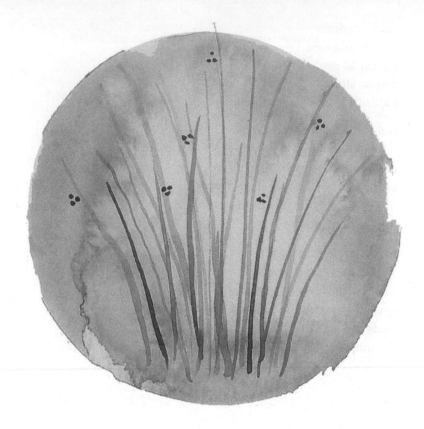

Figure 8. *Juncus effusus*. Small watercolor painting of the species *Juncus effusus*, a type of bulrush used to make Brigid's Crosses in Cape Breton. There are many *Juncus* species that grow wild in Nova Scotia, Canada, often near natural springs. This one grows near the artist's own sacred place. Painting by J. Ellen Cooper.

Brigid's Light

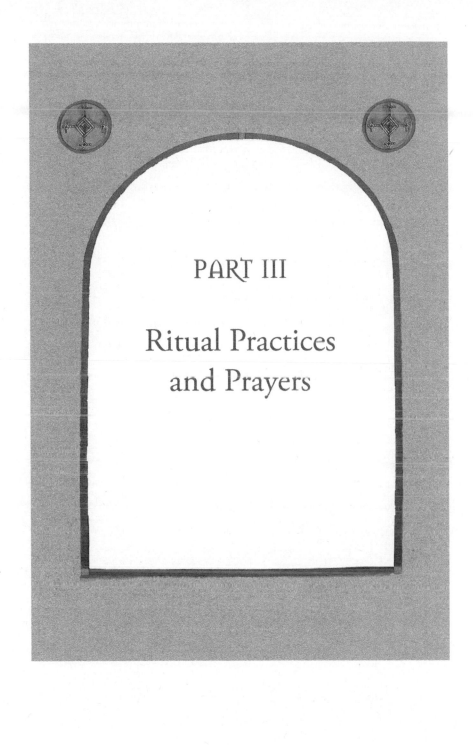

PART III

Ritual Practices and Prayers

Manifesting a Sacred Space for Brigid

Cairelle Crow

I grew up in New Orleans, a city known for many things. It is very Catholic and has a large population of people of Irish descent whose ancestors brought Brigid with them when they emigrated. My earliest awareness of the goddess was as Saint Brigid. When I moved away from Christian-based religions in my late teens and began exploring Paganism and a goddess path, I was surprised and happy to see her familiar name. In my meandering since then, I've worked with many goddesses, some very closely. Brigid was always there as well—sometimes in the background, but never forgotten.

When I began flame-keeping for Brigid, I did so sporadically and usually on a whim when I wanted something. Not the best way to sit in devotion to a goddess! Eventually, through reading, watching, and listening to those much wiser than I, I learned the immense value of engaging in a daily practice, and lighting a flame in devotion to her became second nature. I spent the next two decades learning more about her and working with her. In 2019, I cofounded the Sanctuary of Brigid and dedicated as her priestess.

There have been altars in my life for as long as I can remember, mostly seen in church. But the most meaningful one was in my grandmother's hallway. I knew from an early age that I was not to touch it, but I could look. I recall being mesmerized by the candles and sometimes I heard my grandmother pray in the night when I was supposed to be sleeping. As I got older, I began to notice the intricacies in my grandmother's altar-tending. At the center was a large statue of Mary, heart bleeding, eyes turned upward in supplication, or perhaps in a plea for relief from that which pained her. I used to wonder about her sadness. The altar cloth was changed often, color-coordinated to the season and, sometimes, to a certain purpose.

There was always at least one seven-day candle burning on the altar, and usually more. I always saw small squares of paper tucked beneath the candles, the words frustratingly obscured by the folds. Trinkets and oddities were scattered about—shells, flower petals, hair, small bottles of liquid, honey, and a lipstick tube come to mind. Their placement seemed random, but I knew from watching that they'd been put there with much thought and intent. My grandmother kept this altar for Mary right up until her death in 2001. I am grateful for the early introduction to the tending of a sacred space for a female deity figure, for Mary was much more than the mother of Jesus in my grandmother's home. She was the mother of us all, and she represented the essence of all who mother.

In my own home, I typically have three main altars. One is dedicated to the work I do for myself and others. This is the one I decorate lavishly for the seasons, and it also holds most of the tools I use: chalice, bowl, feather, candles, oils, herbs, waters and dirts, crystals, and more. It's a hodgepodge of activity and gets pretty frenetic at times. Another is my ancestor altar. This holds photos and keepsakes of those I love who are now gone, and it's the place I sit when I want to visit with them. It also holds a black mirror in a frame to represent the unnamed ancestors, and it's where I do work to power up my research for my own family tree and for my genealogy clients who are of a magical nature and who've agreed to this kind of work.

The third altar is the one dedicated to Brigid, and I love it so. It has evolved over the years from a simple cloth and candle into a large space filled with various items that resonate with me and speak to my heart. In the center is a beautiful platter that holds the candles I light for her when it's my turn in the flame-keeping *cill* (a devotional group dedicated to a ritual task), or for when I flame-keep on my own time. On one side sits a gorgeous Paul Borda statue of the three Brigids, assorted framed art, a Saint Brigid's Cross made by my grandson, and a Maman Brigitte doll with a stylized Voodoo look. On the other side there are various crystals, pieces of plants, dried herbs, a swan mug, a small bottle of honey and other items associated with bees, a wire-wrapped carnelian tree, holy water from one of her sacred wells, a bit of mixed dirt picked up from my visits to Ireland, Wales, Scotland, and Cornwall, and other tidbits that I've collected over the years that bring her to mind.

One item in particular is very precious to me—a small mirror in an ornate frame that represents my immigrant ancestors. It was they, and others like them, who brought Brigid to this land. When I flame-keep,

I sometimes catch sight of myself in this mirror, and I am reminded that I am a descendant of those who came from the places where Brigid, as a goddess, is an ancestor of the people. Therefore, I am her daughter as well. When I flame-keep for her, I honor them and myself. The altar I've created for her is especially meaningful to me. When I sit alongside it, I am brought closer to her in my mind and heart.

BUILDING AN ALTAR

I've been asked many times exactly how to create a sacred space for Brigid. It's both an easy and a difficult question to answer, because altars are so individual. Some prefer a simple space—a small table with a plain cloth and a candle. Others use a window ledge or an outdoor space. Still others, like me, love an elaborate space filled with all manner of items that represent Brigid to them. All are correct; all are exactly what is needed.

For those who want to create a sacred space for devotional flame-keeping, or just to honor the goddess, and don't know where to start, the first step is to look within. What's your preferred aesthetic? What can you afford? What other aspects of your lifestyle will affect the space? Small children, pets (especially cats), and inquisitive visitors or roommates can all have an impact on where you decide to set up this private space.

Once you've chosen the best location, consider these two basics for the altar:

- As a way to define the space, use a table covering or a piece of cloth to serve as a base of some sort, in a color that appeals to you. I like white, green, or blue the best, but there's nothing wrong with other colors. I also like cloths with fringe and patterns. Others prefer the simplicity and clean look of a simple white cloth.

- A heat-safe dish or plate on which to place candles so they can burn safely is a necessity. I have a beautifully patterned serving platter that works wonderfully. I've also used a small cauldron with sand in it and a piece of aluminum foil, because that was what I had on hand at the time. And I've stuck a candle into the dirt. Safety first is the rule here. Remember, too, that the aesthetic is secondary to the act of devotion.

The type of candle you choose doesn't matter, as long as it will light and keep burning. In other words, choose what you prefer! I have used all kinds of candles—tapers, small chime or spell candles, five- and seven-day candles, and tea lights. I once used a lighter (that was a short session) and I've lit a fire while camping. The candle color is also a personal choice. I prefer white, but have used orange, green, and blue. Consider sourcing a candle that has been lit from the perpetual flame in Kildare, or the one in Glastonbury. This brings the energy of those flames into the space and continues the perpetual nature of her flame around the world. The Sanctuary of Brigid offers pre-lit candles to anyone who requests one.

How altars are arranged varies widely from person to person. I find it easiest (and safest) to locate candles in the center of the altar, but some prefer placing them to one side or the other. I place Brigid's representative statue in the northeast area of my altar, since that is the direction I associate with her, based on the Wheel of the Year I use in my own practice. I keep some tools in sight and others tucked into a small wooden chest or behind framed art. My altar's aesthetic is based on function—I must be able to do the work with ease—but also on beauty, as it's important to me that I visually enjoy the spaces I create. Each person should consider how their altar will function and manifest their own version of beauty.

CORRESPONDENCES

These lists are not comprehensive and come from my own experiences over the years. The inclusions are what work for *me*. If you resonate with something different than what you find here, follow your own intuition and work with Brigid as you feel inclined.

- Animals: swan, bee, cow, lamb, other domesticated herd animals, serpent, owl, crow, wolf, rabbit, and hibernating animals like badger, bear, and groundhog that emerge around the time of Imbolc

- Best day for spells and other work: Friday

- Colors: red, green, blue, orange, white

- Direction: northeast

- Elements: fire and water

- Essential oils and other scents: chamomile, rosemary, lavender, rose, sage, oakmoss absolute, flower essences and waters

- Food and drink offerings: blackberries, apples, honey, oats, dandelion wine, beer, honey mead

- General associations: fire, hearth, perpetual flame, cauldron, sunrise, wells and springs, embroidery, weaving and quilting, arrows and spears, forge, smithing and metalcrafting, thresholds and doorways, standing-stone formations, cloaks and mantles, corn dollies and the Saint Brigid's Cross, midwifery, domesticated animals, hibernating animals, triskele

- Influences: healing, fertility, abundance, creativity, artistic expressions, writing and poetry, inner strength, protection (especially of women, children, the oppressed and disenfranchised), death and grief, pregnancy, postpartum, fourth trimester, motherhood, friendship, and women's circles

- Metals and gems: gold, brass, copper, silver, carnelian, garnet, moss agate, citrine, red jasper, bumblebee Jasper, emerald

- Planet: Venus

- Plants and flowers: snowdrop, dandelion, trillium, oak tree and acorns, oats, heather, thistle, clover, rushes and straw, wildflowers

- Sacred numbers: 3, 8, 9, and 19

- Time of day: sunrise

Brigid is a multifaceted goddess with whom we can generally work in comfort and ease, and the information offered here may be used as a basis for creating an altar that is personalized to the individual. Also, each person will have their own experiences and opinions, and should always do what works best for them. Take to heart that every sacred space dedicated to her, from the simplest to the most ornate, is surely welcomed when it is created with a loving and devotional intent.

May the light from her flame always guide you to your highest purpose. Bright blessings!

Brigid Invocation

H. Byron Ballard, adapted from Carmichael

Each night and each day, I speak the blessing of Brigid.
I am under the shielding of
Good Brigid each day;
I am under the cloak of
Good Brigid each night.
I am under Her keeping, early and late, every dark, every light.
Brigid is my companion,
Brigid is the maker of song, and of beer.
Brigid is my helping-woman,
My guide, my friend.
May You be offered welcome
And the sweetness of hospitality
By all who hear my voice this day.
Ta failte rohat, a Brid!

Figure 9. *Brigid of Kildare*. Pen and ink on paper, drawn to represent how the artist sees Brigid. The halo behind her head is meant to represent the sun at dawn, illuminating the holiness of Brigid's path. Drawing by Sierra Linder.

Honey and Beeswax Healing Spell

Cairelle Crow

Honey is well-known as a wonderful and effective healer, a blessing and a sacred gift from Mother Earth. Legend speaks of bees traveling back and forth between our world and Brigid's Otherworld apple orchard, carrying back with them what was needed to create magical honey. This spell captures the essence of that sacred bee magic and can be used to heal yourself or for the benefit of others, with their consent.

Materials

> One small, unscented, all-natural beeswax candle
> ¼ teaspoon local-to-you honey
> Candle scribe for carving

Carve the person's name into the candle three times, starting at top near the wick and working your way to the base of the candle. As you carve, envision healing for this person; intend that their illness will decrease as the candle burns. Apply the honey to the base of the candle in a clockwise spiral fashion. Stand the candle in a safe and appropriate holder, then place it on your altar or another sacred space. Light the candle and recite the following:

> Brigid of the Healing Flame,
> Bless [name of the person to be healed] with a quick and full recovery,
> May your honeyed light shine on [name of the person to be healed] and
> Cause only health and a feeling of wellness to remain.

Let the candle burn down and self-extinguish. If you need to snuff it before it's burned down, do so with the intent that you will return and relight it. Once the candle is completely burned down, remove the metal from the wick base, if any, and throw it away. Take the remaining wax and bury it in your yard or in the pot of a houseplant. Repeat as needed. When the desired result is achieved, be sure to light a candle in thanks to Brigid.

Bed Blessing Before Sleep

H. Byron Ballard, adapted from Carmichael

In the name of Brigid,
I stand above my pillow—
Sweetened with lavender and roses,
I stand above my pillow and I bless my head
In the name of Brigid.
I touch my blanket—
Sweetened in the fresh breezes of the morn's dawning,
I touch my blanket and
I bless my body
In the name of Brigid.
I sit upon my bed—
Sweetened with visions of bliss and good health,
I sit upon my bed and
I bless my sleeping
In the name of Brigid.
As pillow comforts head, as blanket warms body, as bed holds me
    safe, in Brigid's loving spirit, I lay me down to sleep.

A Ritual with Brigid

Courtney Weber

I crave. You crave. We crave.

We may crave chocolate, salt, or running off into the hills. The COVID-19 pandemic and subsequent lockdown uncovered our deep, human craving for touch, for connection, for simply being with others.

And what is one of the first things we crave when we sit with others we have not seen in ages? We crave to know how they are, what they have been up to. We crave their stories. In fact, life is made of stories—both individual and collective. We all exist through the stories that are told about us and the stories we tell ourselves about ourselves.

The same is true of the gods. We may describe them by their attributes, or by the mystery cults that may surround them. But we define them personally by the ways in which they touch our lives—by their stories. It is the stories that are told about the gods that keep them alive for us.

Brigid's mythology is packed with beautiful stories. Some depict her as powerful, while some paint her as meek. Others, like the myth in which she is married to Bres, tell us almost nothing about her. Some assume she is a pawn in that story, although there is nothing in it that explicitly says so. Others suggest that she really loved Bres, but we don't have any evidence of that either. All the story truly offers is that, at the end, she is in deep grief over the loss of the son she shared with Bres. Does this story thus mean that Brigid is a goddess of grief?

In other stories, Brigid tricks the powerful, cares for animals, or chases invaders away from her lands. Does this mean that she is a trickster, or a caretaker, or a warrior? What, in fact, is the "true" story, the one that tells us the "truth" of Brigid? The answer is that no single story defines her. They are all simply stories.

Yet it's tempting to try to shape a sort of truth from these tales. That's only human and not, on its own, a crime. But this kind of story-shaping hurts us when we compile our own personal stories—perhaps those etched into our lives by disappointments, embarrassments, failures, and more—and use them to create some kind of "truth" about ourselves. Maybe, after a few romantic disappointments, you've started to believe your story "never has a happy romantic ending." Perhaps some yet unrealized dreams have left you believing your story doesn't include achieving your dreams. At the very least, this kind of storytelling robs you of your joy. It also stunts your potential. Eventually, you'll just crave a new story.

When it's time to release the stories we've believed of ourselves (the ones that hurt us, the ones that aren't true), we can take them to Brigid the healer and Brigid the bard, and maybe even Brigid the smith. She, and they, can help us create something new. The following ritual is designed to do just that.

Materials

Bathtub or shower

A springtime herb easily gotten from your region. Brigid's season is the early spring, so if you can, collect or obtain something that grows in the early spring in your region. Just be sure it's nontoxic, not a protected species, or something to which you have allergies.

Salt

A candle

A piece of tissue paper or paper towel

On the paper, write the stories you no longer wish to live by. An example might be: I am someone who fails in relationships. Or: I am someone who never excels at my work.

Fill the bathtub with water. If you do not have a bathtub, fill a pot of water and bring it to the shower. Combine the salt and herbs into a sachet and soak the sachet in the water. While the herbs are soaking, light the candle and say aloud:

Brigid the Healer, Smith, and Bard,
Fiery woman, powerful guard,
Heal my wounds,

Make me new,
Sinew to sinew,
Root to root.

Take the paper on which you've written the story you want to banish and smush it in the water until it has dissolved, or at least until it is soggy and no longer legible. Set the remains of the old story aside and bathe yourself with the water, envisioning that you are no longer bound by the story. Release the drain (or empty the pot if you are in the shower) and rinse yourself with clean water. Dry yourself with a clean towel and dress in clean clothes.

While the same candle is still burning, take a new piece of paper and write a new story for yourself. For example: I am someone who is lucky in love. Or: I am someone who succeeds at the things I love to do. When finished, fold the paper toward you three times and then say aloud:

Sacred Brigid, Holy Maid,
My lost joy is now repaid.
This is my story, my story true,
Blessed by Brigid, Holy You.

Consider keeping this story in a place where you will come across it regularly—perhaps in a handbag or purse, or a beloved book.

A Prayer to Brighid in Times of Violence

Jenne Micale

Brighid, Lady of Healing, fill us with your peace.
Bring peace to those who hear the crack of thunder from a gun in a
place of refuge, who see the sunlight glint off its barrel.
Brighid, Lady of Healing, fill us with your peace.
Bring peace to those where shots are as common as the cries of spar-
rows, where each step on the crumbling walk is taken with held
breath and a prayer half-believed.
Brighid, Lady of Healing, fill us with your peace.
Bring peace to those who put the softness of their own flesh and the
strength of their bone in the path of the bullet or the blade.
Brighid, Lady of Healing, fill us with your peace.
Bring peace to those with the swift feet or the limping, who flee pain
to preserve life.
Brighid, Lady of Healing, fill us with your peace.
Bring peace to those sheeted in red, the wellspring of their blood
spilling words and meaning on the ground.
Brighid, Lady of Healing, fill us with your peace.
Bring peace to those whose bodies are unmarred, but whose minds
bear the scars of their witness.
Brighid, Lady of Healing, fill us with your peace.
Bring peace to those who stand confused on the shores of the Sunless
Sea, their lives the unplucked apples of the Western Isle, their fare-
wells and jokes and love notes unsaid, unsent.
Brighid, Lady of Healing, fill us with your peace.
Bring peace to those whose tears bear the barge to the Otherworld,
who hold memories in shaking hands and hearts webbed with
cracks.
Brighid, Lady of Healing, fill us with your peace.

Bring peace to those who knit limbs, who tend to souls and hearts,
who offer the bread of comfort and the milk of nurturance.
Brighid, Lady of Healing, fill us with your peace.
Bring peace to those who bear witness, who share the words of truth
and so drive off the black wings of silence and its carrion crow
with their telling.
Brighid, Lady of Healing, fill us with your peace.
Bring peace to those who fire the gun and loft the grenade, to those
who maim and those who kill, so that the fire of their rage is
quenched in your well's sweet waters.
Brighid, Lady of Healing, fill us with your peace.
Let your waters pour out with the peace of the singing brook scatter-
ing sunlight, the peace of the roaring white-maned sea, the peace
of the drumming rain and the lake ringed with reeds.
Brighid, Lady of Healing, fill us with your peace.
Let your waters knit wounds and quell the blaze of rage, of pain, the
starless deep of despair and the gray slate of indifference.
Brighid, Lady of Healing, fill us with your peace.
Let us swim in your healing waters until we know that we are all
enfolded in the same sea, that we are the sea itself, the sea coursing
through the salt of our tears and of our blood, turned sweet by
your palms into the deep well of compassion.
Brighid, Lady of Healing, fill us with your peace.

Walking Brigid's Path—A Tarot Spread

Nancy Hendrickson

Brigid, at least in legend, was a woman unlike any walking the earth today. She was reported to be a warrior, a poet, a healer, and a smith. Her abilities were as varied as the names by which she was known—Brede, Brigit, Brigandu, the Triple Goddess, Mary of the Gael, and the Bright Arrow. She has even been likened to the Roman goddess Brigantia.

According to Irish lore, Brigid was constantly occupied in promoting the good of others; she cleansed lepers and restored sight to a person who was blind from birth. An old Irish song found in *Poets and Dreamers: Studies and Translations from the Irish* claimed that "Brigid's kiss was sweeter than the whole of the waters of Lough Erne; or the first wheaten flour, worked with fresh honey into dough" (Charles Scribner's Sons, 1903). Brigid could talk to the animals, work magic on a sunbeam, and cause food and drink to increase, just as Jesus did with the fishes and loaves. Brigid in all her guises—goddess, woman, and saint—walked a path that calls out to us, even today.

Walking Brigid's Path is a tarot spread that creates a connection between you and the many facets of the goddess. Whoever appears in your spread is the Brigid you are most called to work with at this time. May she be the one for whom you wish.

To begin, shuffle the entire deck, then deal seven cards facedown in the indicated positions (see Figure 10). The cards are interpreted as follows:

1. My fire spirit—In what way am I the smith at the forge? What am I creating?

2. My healer spirit—How do I heal myself and others?

3. My warrior spirit—For what am I willing to fight?

4. My craft spirit—How do I or should I spend time perfecting my craft?

5. Brigid's gift to me—What is my unique gift?

6. My path forward—What path is now open to me?

7. Brigid's blessing—Be open to receiving a special blessing from Brigid.

As each card is turned up, consider not only the card, but how it connects to Brigid. For example, if you drew the Nine of Swords in position 1, how might Brigid bring her fire arrow to bear on your worries? Alternatively, if your path forward is one of great challenge, call on Brigid the warrior to show you the way to courage. If the action asked of you is unclear, draw additional cards for clarification.

After you've completed the spread, journal the advice found in each of the seven cards. Then consider adopting the persona of Brigid the poet and craft a short verse about your path moving forward, perhaps like the one below.

May Brigid be with you.

The Blessing of the Fields
For the wheat,
the grapes, the pomegranates.
I give thanks.
For the companions,
and the craft.
For the map
without borders.
I am blessed.

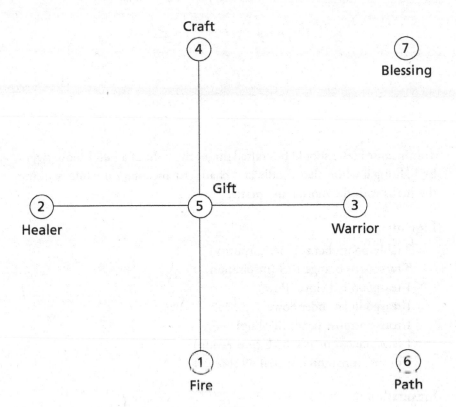

Figure 10. Walking Brigid's Path tarot spread.

Brigid's Altar Incense

Jim "Raven" Stefanowicz

This incense blend should be crafted under the light of a Full Moon. Begin by lighting a white altar candle and chant the incantation while working the herbs with the mortar and pestle.

Ingredients

    3 tablespoons benzoin resin (purity)
    3 teaspoons orange peel (inspiration)
    1 teaspoon red clover (love)
    1 teaspoon lavender flowers (peace)
    1 teaspoon rose petals (healing)
    1 teaspoon white oak bark (protection)
    3 drops cinnamon essential oil (power)

Incantation

    This blend I bless by pestle and mortar,
    By the Lady of Fire and Sacred Water.
    Awaken now, Great Spirits of the Green,
    In the name of Brigid, Goddess and Queen.
    To consecrate and bless the air,
    By the magick of Kildare.

Three Times Three

Holly Devanna

I have always been drawn to Brigid's fire.

When I found my way into the world of Celtic mythology in my twenties, I was utterly enchanted by the luminous goddess Brigid in her different forms. As bard, healer, and smith, she seamlessly embodied all the qualities I yearned to express in my own magical, mythopoetic life. I was in my thirties when I really settled into my purpose as a creatrix, and I felt Brigid's influence shining in from all the margins of my life. Since then, I've felt a calling to paint her and bring her to life, but her form has remained elusive for many years as she has quietly worked her magic on me from the Otherworld.

It wasn't until recently, when I began working with my husband as a jeweler and metalsmith, that I truly felt Brigid's creative fire being channeled through my heart and hands. Brigid holds a special place in my spiritual world—as keeper of the flame, as wielder of hammer and anvil, and as whispering muse behind my words. Though my passion for writing has always come in fits and starts throughout most of my life, running the gamut between poetry, novellas, nonfiction, and instruction, her bardic spirit informs my words in whatever shape they take.

When we crafted a special collection of jewelry featuring triskeles, triquetras, and lunulas in the spring of 2021, this verse flowed straight from the muse to the paper. It is meant to be spoken as a charm over the jewelry we craft by hammer and hand, and to bring blessings to its wearer. But really it is a charm that carries Brigid's magic into any talisman you may wish to carry.

Three times three and shades of green,
By meadow, forge, and sacred spring,
A charm is made these worlds between.

The harp fills emerald fields with song,
While hammer blows come swift and strong,
To this talisman may luck belong.

As winds the rolling hills caress'd,
May fortune to them manifest,
Who wears what Brigid's hands hath bless'd.

I invite you to speak this charm to empower your own talismans. May these humble verses invoke Brigid's unique magic for you.

Priestess Invocation for Brigid's Return

Lynne Sedgmore

Hail Brigid
Your quickening of spring returns
Deep within the wisdom of the land
Deep within each one of us

We are your greening
Enlivened by your fire
Wings awakening wide
Expanding into flight
We are your swans heralding the light
Hearts twinkling in innocent delight
Souls singing poetry
Healing through your love

Hail Brigid
Goddess of the hearth and forge
Bringer of the Celtic way
We are your quickening
Your Priestesses in the world today

Figure 11. *Light Anchoring*. Swan encounter at the Japanese Gardens in Kildare, Ireland—a sacred moment. The photos were conceived as part of a visual story and as an individual window into the liminal world. Photo by Chantal Simon.

A Spell for Ireland's Lost Daughters

Yeshe Matthews

Maybe you don't know much about your heritage, or perhaps you have a broken family connection that makes your Irish lineage complicated. Maybe you're new to magic and you don't know where to begin. Maybe you've felt a little worried that you might not be "Irish enough" to receive Brigid's grace. Whatever the reason, if you'd like to connect with Brigid and your Irish heritage, try this spell.

On January 31st, take a strip of cloth, and say these words over it:

> Brigid, cloak me in your magic. I am your daughter, and I place
> myself at your feet.

Tie the piece of cloth on your clothesline, a tree, or somewhere else near your home, and leave a pat of butter beneath it as an offering. Starting on February 1st, and for the next nineteen days, light a tea light or candle each day and repeat the prayer at your altar.

On the twentieth day, pour an offering of milk and leave yellow flowers for Brigid at your altar. Light a tea light, but say nothing. Then watch for her signs.

Elemental Blessing

Mary Tidbury

By mist and by rain
By jewels of the sea
Remember my darling
That you're part of me.

By breeze and by gale
By winds wild and free
Remember my darling
That you're part of me.

By spark and by flame
By the fire's ecstasy
Remember my darling
That you're part of me.

By root and by bud
By leaf and by tree
Remember my darling
You are part of me.

PART IV

Goddess of Hearth
and Home

Cooking for Brigid

Dawn Aurora Hunt

My kitchen is a sacred space. Like most kitchen witches, the magic I've cooked up over the years, from bubbling soups, roasted meats, quiet cups of tea, and sabbat dinners, lingers in every corner. The warmth of the hearth—or in the modern witch's kitchen, the oven—burns low and slow all year round. As the Wheel of the Year turns, my meals change with the seasons. Since seasonal and devotional cooking is such a huge part of my practice, each season brings with it a host of new flavors, spell-workings, and celebrations of the gods.

One of my favorite times of year to be a kitchen witch is at Imbolc. When I am celebrating Brigid, there is a special note of warmth in all my workings. I feel it in the steady hum of a slow cooker simmering up thick stew, in the smell of toasty bread baking, and in the spiced honey stirred into ginger tea.

Growing up in a traditional Italian Catholic family meant that Saint Brigid was a name I heard once a year at church. But I never gave her much thought until I found a Pagan path and was reintroduced to her as the goddess Brigid. In my early workings with her, I learned of her associations with hearth, home, fires, and livestock. All of these things are deeply rooted in my personal practice. Because kitchen witchery is an everyday practice of mindfulness and magic, keeping Brigid hearthside in my kitchen has become important to my magical workings, especially in early spring. Here in the northeastern United States, the cold winter months keep a grip on us well into April. Inviting Brigid to warm our homes and hold the flames of Imbolc bright in our minds helps the cold months pass and prompts a renewed anticipation of spring.

Every year at Imbolc, in honor of Brigid, we light candles (or a huge fire in the backyard, weather permitting) and share a feast of hearty foods associated with the goddess to warm our bodies, hearts, and souls. Using ingredients that are sacred to Brigid—beef, milk, honey, and thyme—we invite the goddess to join our celebration. Here are some of the dishes we dedicate to the goddess.

SHEPHERD'S PIE

This hearty one-dish beef pie is topped with whipped potatoes and filled with flavor. Potatoes have grounding energy, and ingredients like milk, butter, and ground beef are all associated with joy, kinship, and, of course, cattle, which Brigid held sacred. You can also substitute lamb for all or some of the beef for a more authentic flavor. Combining these ingredients with the energetic powers of herbs like rosemary for peace, thyme for knowledge, and bay leaf for psychic awareness makes this a spiritually and energetically powerful dish that can be shared around the table and around the circle.

Ingredients for the topping

    5 pounds yellow potatoes

    1 cup milk

    6 tablespoons butter

    Salt and pepper to taste

Ingredients for the filling

    2 pounds lean ground beef

    1 white onion, chopped

    3 cloves garlic, chopped

    2 large carrots, chopped

    1 tablespoon cornstarch

    1 can (4 oz) tomato paste

    1 cup beef stock

    2 teaspoons Worcestershire sauce

    1 teaspoon dried thyme (or 1 tablespoon fresh)

    3 whole bay leaves

    1 teaspoon dried rosemary (or 1 tablespoon fresh)

    1 8-oz package frozen peas

1 8-oz package frozen corn
Salt and pepper to taste

Fill a large saucepan with water and set on the stove at medium/low heat. Wash and peel the potatoes, cut them into cubes, and place them in the water. Bring to a boil. Periodically test the potatoes with a fork while they are boiling. When a fork can be inserted easily and the potatoes begin to fall apart slightly, remove them from the heat and drain. In the same pan, add milk, butter, salt, and pepper. With an electric mixer on low, whip the potatoes until creamy and all the ingredients are well mixed. If the potatoes are too dry, add more milk and/or butter by the tablespoonful until the desired texture is achieved. Set aside.

Preheat the oven to 400° F. In a large, deep skillet, cook the ground beef, onions, garlic, and carrots together until the meat is no longer pink and the onions are soft. Add the cornstarch and stir until dissolved. Add the tomato paste, beef stock, Worcestershire sauce, thyme, bay leaves, and rosemary. Cover, reduce the heat to low, and simmer for 20 minutes, or until the liquid has been reduced by half.

Uncover and stir in the frozen peas and corn. Pour the mixture into a large glass or ceramic baking dish (13 x 9 inches). Top with the mashed potatoes, being sure to cover the top completely so the filling doesn't bubble and spill out. Place the baking dish on a cookie sheet to prevent spillage in the oven. Cook for 30–45 minutes until the top is golden brown. Enjoy hot with cornmeal biscuits and spiced honey butter.

CORNMEAL BISCUITS

These biscuits go well with shepherd's pie, especially when topped with spiced honey butter.

Ingredients

¾ cup milk
2 tablespoons cider vinegar
1 cup flour
¾ cup fine-ground yellow cornmeal
2 tablespoons sugar
1 teaspoon salt
1 tablespoon baking powder
1 teaspoon baking soda
1 stick of cold butter
1 cup shredded cheddar cheese (optional)

Preheat the oven to 425° F. In a small bowl, combine the milk and vinegar, stir well, and set aside. This will begin to curdle, creating a "butter milk." Allow it to stand for at least 5 minutes.

Meanwhile, in a large bowl, whisk together the flour, cornmeal, sugar, salt, baking powder, and baking soda. Using your hands or two butter knives cut the butter into the dry ingredients. Work the cold butter in until the mixture is clumpy, and the butter is consistently pea-sized. Add cheese if desired. Pour in the milk mixture and stir gently until the dough becomes shaggy and sticks together. Gently work the dough into a rectangle about one inch thick, then fold the dough like a letter, creating three distinct layers.

Gently roll the dough with a rolling pin or press the dough slightly with your hands until it is again one inch thick; repeat the process of folding and rolling. Use a 2-inch biscuit cutter or the top of a drinking glass to cut out biscuits, being sure to coat the cutter or top of the glass with flour before each cut. Refold and roll out any extra dough to get more biscuits. Place the cut biscuits on a parchment-lined baking sheet and bake 12–15 minutes, until tops are golden brown. Enjoy warm or at room temperature.

Figure 12. Makings of an Imbolc feast for Brigid. Photo by Dawn Aurora Hunt.

SPICED HONEY BUTTER

This spiced honey butter makes a perfect topping for cornmeal biscuits. It can also be used to add a sweet and spicy flavor to just about anything.

Ingredients

> 1 stick butter, softened
> 1 teaspoon honey
> 1 teaspoon maple syrup
> 1 teaspoon cinnamon
> Pinch nutmeg
> Pinch ground ginger
> Pinch smoked paprika (optional)

In a medium bowl, combine all ingredients and stir until they are well mixed and no lumps remain. Refrigerate until ready to use. Keep in an airtight container for up to a month in the refrigerator.

As We Smoor the Candle

H. Byron Ballard, adapted from Carmichael

I am smooring the candle
As Brigid would smoor it.
Blessed be the house, blessed be the hearth, blessed be the people all!

Bridie's Bedtime Milk

Cairelle Crow

This simple recipe for a warm and comforting bedtime drink comes from my grandmother, Mabel Norma Taylor, who got it from her own grandmother, Ada Bridie Carter Taylor. My granny was very proud of her Scottish and Irish roots. As a child, I was served a mug of this milk every evening before bed. I sipped and listened as my grandmother shared stories of our family from days gone by. It is one of my favorite childhood memories.

The tradition continues, as I now make this treat for my grandchildren to sip while I share my own stories with them.

Ingredients

    1½ cups of milk
    ¼ teaspoon of vanilla extract
    1 teaspoon of honey (Check with a licensed medical provider
        before giving honey to very small children)
    A pinch of nutmeg for sprinkling (optional)

Warm the milk on a low flame (or in the microwave) until very warm, but not boiling. Pour into a mug, stir in the vanilla and honey, and top with a sprinkle of nutmeg. Enjoy!

Brighid of the Outcasts

Jenne Micale

Write me a poetry of the undeserving—
of those huddled at shadowed fires far from the garth
who eye the palisades suspiciously
and earn their names battling our noblest of sons.

Sing too of their ragged women, unbeautiful
and veiled from our honest gaze, or naked sows
sucking generations of war! Or weaponed
and solitary, faces painted with lampblack.

"We speak no such guttural tongues here," you say,
from the timbered safety of your hut, full-bellied
and fire-warmed, rightful inheritor of soil and blood.
Behind this wall, there is culture. Breach it,

And feast only on the raw, scrabbling in dirt,
fit only for chains. You see not your own smallness
under those darkening boughs, the tumble of
history toward its inevitable end.

Meanwhile, the bright Lady leaves your tidy hearth
for that wilder one woven of elder twigs
and desperation. Nameless, she accepts the gifts
offered by a trembling hand, whispered, worried, hushed.

She gives to them her Father's sword, the kind milk
poured from the red-eared cow, the pillar of a hand
on a weakening back, the shaft of sunlight
through gem-green leaves. She asks nothing in return.

"This is a greater temple," she says, "than those
with their forests of roof beams and pillared stones."
She asks nothing of deserving, lighting the flame—
a fragile spark of heaven in the shadowed yard.

Brigid's Blackberry Crumble

Laura Louella

On warm summer mornings in July, I like to walk along the river and pick blackberries. As sure as the seasons turn, they are waiting for me each year, and I am grateful. It takes me back to a time when my grandparents and I picked fruit for the delicious cobblers my grandma made. I remember being in the kitchen with her, making fruit cobblers, while my grandpa was on the back porch churning vanilla ice cream. Those were sweet days that I cherish. I carry this love in my heart and I know it is a gift from Brigid.

There is nothing better than talking with Brigid about how life is going, petitioning her with prayers for family and friends while I pick berries. I approach this job of gathering the berries just as I do my life—with reverence and appreciation. If I am not thoughtful as I choose the fruit, I will be scratched by the plant and it will hurt and burn. As in life, when I rush ahead and don't pay attention to the details, I find myself being reminded with unpleasant surprises. With thoughtfulness, I pick this beautiful fruit from its thorny branches. These brambling vines remind me that there is always beauty in life, even when the thorns are poking and scratching me. There is a lesson to be learned here: Working toward something lovely cannot be taken for granted. I thank Brigid for blessing me with these wonderful blackberries. They are so juicy as they come off the vine and I can't resist popping a few into my mouth. I love their sweetness, and the tart ones too!

Once home, I wash the berries and lay them out to dry. Their deep colors of black and purple with a touch of red remind me of colors on a painter's palette. They are intensely beautiful.

I always look forward to sharing this dessert with my family. Carrying on family traditions is very important to me. It's how I honor those who came before me and it's how I teach my children about our resilient ancestors who, much like the blackberry bramble, persevered under harsh conditions to nourish us.

Ingredients

6 tablespoons cold unsalted butter
¾ cup walnuts or pecans, your choice
¼ cup firmly packed brown sugar
A dash of cinnamon
½ cup flour
¼ teaspoon salt
¼ cup oats
6 cups of blackberries

Preheat the oven to 350° F. Place six ramekins on a cookie sheet lined with foil, or use a silicone mat. Slice the butter and return it to refrigerator until ready to use.

Place the walnuts or pecans, brown sugar, and cinnamon in a small food processor and pulse briefly to grind the nuts. You will be grinding a bit more as ingredients are added, so don't grind too much at this step.

Add the flour and salt, then pulse again to mix. Add the cold butter and pulse again to combine all the ingredients. When it begins to look crumbly, transfer to a large bowl and gently fold in the oats. Hand mix to create large buttery crumbs.

Fill each ramekin about ¾ full with blackberries, then add the butter crumble on top of the berries to fill each ramekin. Place the ramekins in the oven and bake for 30–35 minutes.

Once done, remove from the oven, serve with vanilla ice cream, and enjoy your sweet summer evening.

Remember to thank Brigid!

Sacred Flame

Jim "Raven" Stefanowicz

Brigid of the Healing Waters,
Brigid of the Sacred Flame,
Come to us, your sons and daughters,
As we call your name.
Weave for us your magick spell,
By standing stone and chalice well,
Spark of Kildare's Fire come to us.

Brigid, Lady of the Hearth
Brigid, heal the Earth.

Be to us a shining vision,
Be to us a font of life,
Mend for us the world's division,
Turning darkness into light.
You of life, death, and rebirth,
Our Fertile Mother of the Earth,
From womb to tomb be with us all the while,
You, the joy within a newborn's smile.

Brigid, Lady of the Hearth
Brigid, heal the Earth.

They thought they had snuffed out your flame,
But too enduring was your name.
You lived within the hearts of all your people.
Gentle Lady of the Lake,
Take your mighty sword and break
The chains and pains of all your faithful children,
Take this world of clay and rebuild it.

Brigid, Lady of the Hearth
Brigid, heal the Earth.

Refrigerator Pickles for Brigid

Rev. Rayna Templebee

Water and fire, water and fire, water and fire—these two major aspects of Brigid came together for me first in the kitchen. Specifically my grandmother's kitchen, which was bigger, better equipped, and much calmer than the small kitchen where my parents hurriedly cooked their meals. The way Grandma Marge moved calmly through the kitchen space, controlling every aspect of how we ate and what we ate, and especially the way she combined all manner of mysterious ingredients, gave me my first appreciation of magick.

Grandma Marge seemed to be inspired by her time in the kitchen, and her recipe box was filled with scraps of paper where, with the handwriting of an English teacher, she neatly wrote out the ingredients, directions, and source of each particular spell. She taught me to be creative in the kitchen, like Brigid, but also disciplined—to measure carefully and cook with care. I still associate this kind of controlled creativity with the domain of Brigid—the ability of the well-trained artist to create without causing chaos, the perfectly honed skills of the master craftswoman.

While Grandma Marge taught me to cook, she told stories about her family, her lineage, and what it meant to be Scots-Irish. She was my only grandparent whose family had spent significant time in this country. All the others were born in Central Europe or their parents emigrated from there. Her sister did the research to join the Daughters of the American Revolution and, even though it had been centuries since her people (the Maxwells, Lamberts, and Hannays) had left County Mayo and nearby parts of Ireland to settle in the Midwest farm belt, she clung tightly to her Scots-Irish identity, as my mother does today. I think that, to her, it meant being a self-reliant person, an independent thinker, and someone not too tightly controlled by the Church. There were no saints in her house, but Brigid was alive in the tradition of the fierce, caring women who took charge of their families, even when they were sometimes fragile themselves.

Sundays were not about organized religion in Grandma Marge's house. My grandfather begged her to go to church to quiet the gossips in their small town, but she (and he as well, to be fair) preferred to be outdoors on Sundays, or in the kitchen. Our holy day was filled with long walks to see the wildflowers that she addressed by name, pointing out how the fae lived in lady slippers and telling us that the lily of the valley were their little hats. Then we read poetry on a big rock by the river, until it was finally time to bring the fire and water—fire and water, fire and water—of Brigid's energy together in the kitchen. A huge feast of fried chicken, many kinds of cabbage slaw, potato salad, refrigerator pickles, asparagus from the garden, some kind of mysterious jello salad, and plenty of alcohol for the adults completed the perfect day.

Grandma Marge, her mother Big Grandma Fontaine, and my mother moved with what seemed perfect coordination around the kitchen, frying and peeling and mixing simultaneously, while directing me in whatever small low-stakes tasks I could manage. Their inspiration was the delight of bringing family together. They introduced me to Brigid as the creative spark that keeps a woman cooking with joy after decades of doing that very same thing every night of the week. I learned that Brigid was my portal to the past, to the generations of Scots-Irish women who left their homeland and not only made do in a new land, but created deliciousness and laughter wherever they went.

These women shared their food magick with other women and created community. They mastered the transformation of water and fire that is pickling, preserving, canning, and baking. They showed their love through preparing the favorite foods of each child, each grandchild, and each demanding husband. The kitchen was their holy temple, decorated with small feminine ornaments like teacups, a cherished dishware pattern, and the well-worn magickal tools they used to mash and chop and fry. I was fortunate enough to inherit an electric frying pan from Grandma Marge. It is one of my most prized possessions, because it radiates power from the many meals prepared by her loving hands.

There is magick and holiness in food prepared with love. Brigid's well is never empty, and her sacred waters nourish not only our bodies, but also our spirits. My relationship with Brigid grows stronger each time I cook with inspiration, with love, and with spirit. When I master the alchemy of transforming water into stew or flour into cake, when I harness fire to water, I am standing at the place Brigid holds for me. It is a place of power and authority I learned to assume by hovering around my grandmothers, watching their ritualized movements while they read from cryptic books covered in drips and drabs of unknown potent substances.

Brigid is the fire in my head that inspires a new meal. She is the cool water that fills my belly. And she is the compassion and care that I put into feeding friends and family. Here is one of my favorite recipes from Grandma Marjorie Lambert—refrigerator pickles for Brigid.

Ingredients

   2 cups sugar
   2 cups vinegar
   1 tablespoon salt
   1 teaspoon turmeric
   1 teaspoon ground cloves
   6 small pickling cucumbers, sliced
   1 egg-sized onion, sliced
   1 small green pepper from the garden, sliced

Bring the vinegar, sugar, and salt to a boil, then add the spices. Cook the cucumbers, onion, and pepper in the liquid until clear and tender. Refrigerate and enjoy anytime. They will last all summer.

Brighid of the Melting Snow

Jenne Micale

Maybe that's my sacrifice, my bare feet
in the snow with the cold burning as coals
in the hearth, the blue hurting flame of the heart
that fires everything, the engine of ourselves.

The heat of me melts the snow underfoot
as I, singing your welcome, slide my way in
over the slick iced sheet of the floor, hands
catching the doorframe, but still I sing it,

unfallen, unfaltering, the basket of
your bed welcoming you to our hearth, this place,
every place you touch. You don't mind my sodden
slippers. You don't mind the messy floor. Welcome

to your bed, our bed, every bed rush-woven,
to your fire, our fire, every fire in kitchen
or stone-walled hearth or even a hot plate
in a rented room. You are everywhere

there is warmth, the summer of our breath
the slow burn of fire and flesh curled against us,
the heat of ourselves melting the winter
the ice rivering under our naked feet.

Brigid's Cloak

Jamie Della

Menses and magick arrived in my life in the summer of 1979. I was eleven and a half years old when our parents put my younger sister, Julie, and me on a southbound train headed for a two-week stay with Uncle David and Aunt Sadie, while my parents took a second honeymoon in Spain.

I held my little sister's cold and sweaty hand in my own as we looked for seats, struck by a stab of loneliness because I was without my mother's protection for the first time in my life. I sat down and leaned my head against the window, watching orange orchards whip by the windows. The diagonal rows of round green trees laden with plump Valencia and navel oranges made patterns like a chessboard.

At the edge of the orchards, eucalyptus trees swayed razor-sharp leaves, flaps of bark, and stringy branches. I stared at the aromatic pods, willing their camphor scent to help me breathe through my fear. My aunt and uncle were hippies who smoked pot and lived in the country. Nobody ever acted so free, so outside of the law, in the land of the Republicans where I lived in central Orange County, California, birthplace of Richard Nixon and last home of John Wayne.

The landscape outside the window opened up suddenly, as we cruised on a track so close to the Pacific Ocean that you could watch the surfers and playful dolphins—all from the soft comfort of our cushioned seats. I stared at the haze on the horizon and wondered if I could be carefree enough to shuck the heavy cloak of societal dos and don'ts that weighed me down.

When the train pulled into Oceanside, Aunt Sadie ran to us with open arms. She wore purple sunglasses, which she pushed up onto her curly auburn hair, flashing bright green eyes of welcome.

I tried to memorize the road to their house, just in case I needed to trace my way back—kind of like a mental trail of breadcrumbs that comforted me. Two exits toward the mountains from the freeway. When we arrived at their home, luscious smells of tuberose, honeysuckle, and neroli shook me out of my fear, weaving green tendrils around my anxiety until it dissolved into wonder and joy.

Here I could roam free through two acres of unspoiled land with a winding path that led through a jungle of overhanging trees to a black-bottomed pool and a redwood deck where my cousins, sister, and I sunned on lounge chairs. We spent hours in Aunt Sadie's walk-in closet, adorning ourselves with gossamer dresses, gauzy scarves, and dangling earrings.

And then one morning, cramps clutched at my stomach. In horror, I felt a warm liquid exiting my body and watched as the stain of a brilliant magenta flower bloomed on the starched white sheets. I feared that I would get in trouble, squeezed my thighs together, and told my sister that my stomach hurt. Everyone went to breakfast but me. I cleaned myself up the best I could, threw a towel over the stain, and crawled back into bed. Finally, Aunt Sadie arrived with a pot of chamomile tea and a cup, as I hoped she would. By some ancestral instinct, via a thin line of Scottish blood in my veins, I knew hot water and herbs made medicine.

Aunt Sadie rubbed that ultrasensitive hairline at my temples with a gentle touch. Shivers caused the tears rimming my eyes to fall onto my cheeks. She told me how scared she had been when her father announced they would leave Scotland for the Americas.

"I was nine years old and the eldest of four children," Aunt Sadie recalled in her singsong voice. "I should have been the bravest, but all I could think about was how I would miss the faeries. We had tea parties when I crossed the moor to my grandparents' home."

Aunt Sadie was so casual in her tone when she talked about meeting the faeries, as if she had mentioned a deer or rabbit that had been trusting enough to approach a child in nature. As humans, we can almost understand telepathy with dogs, cats, and even hawks or robins. But communing with elemental creatures of spirit, of wind and flowers, of rivers and trees, had never occurred to me before as something that other people understood. Yet, although I had never actually seen a magickal, elemental spirit, the idea of having tea with a faerie slowly sank into my awareness as a truth as tangible as gravity.

I felt wide awake and brave as I listened to Aunt Sadie describe emerald-green hills that stretched as far as the eye could see. "Those hills are the cloak of Brigid, the goddess of Ireland and Scotland. You can bring her cloak, which comforts and protects and nurtures, wherever you go," Aunt Sadie murmured as she pulled the handmade afghan over my shoulders.

Aunt Sadie's tales about the faeries of the moor and legends of Brigid fell upon me like rose petals and, soon, I fell asleep.

The second time I met Brigid was at an Imbolc celebration at the home of Jeannette Reynolds, a small blond woman whose eyes sparkled like Queen Titania herself. This ancient observance, which marks the beginning of spring, is also known as Brigid's Day. As I passed between the trees that led to the front yard where Jeannette held her Pagan ceremonies, I looked up and saw the word "Remember" painted on a wooden sign. Many years later when I mentioned the sign to Jeannette, she said there never had been a sign like that—that I saw what the fae folk and Brigid wanted me to see. She said I was on the cusp of my Saturn Return—a coming of age that is often followed by major life changes—and the doorway to my spiritual life had been flung open. They wanted me to remember who I was.

Jeannette lit the bonfire and began the ceremony by requesting the attendance and protection of the Four Directions. Then she called upon Brigid as a goddess of the hearth, patroness of fire, poetry, and smithcrafting, as she sprinkled rose petals on the ground in a circle of protection around those gathered.

As I stared at the dancing flames, Jeannette explained that Brigid is the flash of inspiration and the constancy of hope. Her fire forges daggers and shields so that the goddess's protection is as soft and nurturing as a favorite blanket, but also as sharp and aggressive as a sword.

Suddenly, I felt a yearning to turn my pen into a sword. I lit candles in Brigid's honor. I longed to visit her sacred wells and tap into her creative inspiration. In the process of my devotions, I cast a spell to become a writer. Within a short time, the literary agent for whom I worked as an assistant told me an editor was looking for a writer to create a Wicca cookbook. Here was my chance to write about the power of hearth magick and how cooking was a tangible, nurturing celebration of the Pagan sabbats found on the Wheel of the Year. Grateful as a child unwrapping a most-wished-for birthday present, I began looking for a home away from home where I could write while my husband or a sitter took care of my sons.

Brigid's Light

Tea and Sympathy, a Celtic tea shop, was the perfect location to invoke magick and find inspiration. After I had several feverish writing sessions fueled by hot tea and scones heaped high with Devonshire cream, Nancy, the shop owner, asked me what I was working on. She brightened up when I told her that I was writing a cookbook based on the ancient Celtic holidays. Nancy invited me to join her traveling store, a booth that followed the circuit of Celtic festivals, Scottish Highland games, and Irish fairs.

Less than a year later, I was seated at the Tea and Sympathy booth next to female authors who wrote historical romance novels featuring swashbuckling rebel Scots and Irishmen and strongheaded women, very much like *The Outlander* series written by Diana Gabaldon. In fact, Amanda Scott, the most successful author Nancy had enlisted, wrote nearly thirty books that gave Diana fierce competition back in the day.

It was the early 2000s—not an easy time to be an out-of-the-closet witch. I surmised that a tie to Celtic history provided my best chance to convey the wisdom of earth spirituality without scaring people. I bought a tartan scarf and a glittering faery pin to hold the rosette in place that honored my 1/16th Scottish blood. I lamented that I wasn't Celtic enough to my fellow authors, who wrote about the clans to which they belonged. Could I really honor Brigid with such a small amount of the bloodline?

Then one day, a festival, which happened to take place a few blocks from my Uncle David and Aunt Sadie's home, held its opening ceremony quite close to the Tea and Sympathy booth. The bagpipes wailed and began a soulful tune. Immediately, a vision appeared in my mind's eye. I was sailing on a ship with my fellow villagers and family. Soot covered our faces and clothes as we watched the British army set our thatched roofs aflame. The cold spray rose from a black sea as we sailed south, forced to leave our homes with little more than what we could carry in our hands.

Tears streamed down my face as I turned to author Kathleen Givens, a Dark Irish type with jet-black hair and piercing blue eyes. "What was that song?" I whispered.

"The Scottish national anthem," she replied, putting her hand on my shoulder.

"I saw us . . . sailing from our home," I whispered. I began to cry in earnest as the images roiled around in my head like memories aflame.

"There's your proof, darling. The Scottish blood runs true through you."

I took ragged breaths as the bagpipers marched by our booth; their music sharpened into the sword that continues to fight for Brigid's honor.

As I reached my thirty-third year, the desire to know Brigid more intimately began to burn like a candle that could not be extinguished. I had published two books on witchcraft that were selling well, and I took every opportunity to promote the Craft. I craved the fullness of my potential as a witch author with a fervor that caused me to carve a crescent moon in my side gate and paint a large sun and a six-foot goddess in my kitchen. Together with my young sons, I tended the herb garden and decorated seasonal altars with crystals, candles, hand-dyed silk cloths, and objects found in nature.

If I could keep the momentum of my success going, it seemed possible that I might break the barriers between the mainstream culture and magick. I could help witches to stop feeling isolated and scared. I could spread the goddess faith and elevate the Divine Feminine. For myself personally, I wanted to leave an unhappy marriage. But I feared I would lose a custody battle solely because I was a witch if I ever chose to divorce.

The small window that made my freedom a possibility occurred one hot August morning, when a producer from the Sci-Fi Channel, later known as Syfy, called to ask if I would be interested in hosting a kitchen witch television show. I was thrilled. All my energy, attention, words, and deeds went into my desire to debunk myths about witches and gain my own liberation. Despite on-camera jitters, I felt like a beacon of golden-white light flecked with angelic shades of blue.

But two weeks after filming, the World Trade Center was attacked and the show, named *The Cauldron*, was canceled. But by that time, I was already out of the broom closet. Even my son's kindergarten teacher knew I practiced witchcraft. So I held up my head, stuck out my chin, and pushed through with Capricornian tenacity, writing several more books, earnestly waiting and casting spells for my next big break.

The only time I felt that I was truly myself was at Pagan gatherings. We spoke a language all our own about the power of symbols, astrology, herbal medicine, animal totems, and universal influences. We talked about setting intentions for moon rituals, the large chunk of black tourmaline we had just bartered, and powerful drumming ceremonies. Glitter seemed a constant companion for me. And yet I wondered if "it," my chance, would ever return.

One year, at the Women's Spirit Winter Solstice festival, I was signing my magickal books in the booth of a witch's shop, making the transition from the relatively mainstream Celtic world to the full-fledged goddess and witch community. New witchlings, blossoming mothers, enchantresses, queens, crones, and hags sauntered or strolled by, like a parade of elemental beings gathered for their Pagan holiday. They looked as if they had been shopping in Aunt Sadie's closet. At the back of her booth space, the elder high priestess of the Crimson Dragon Druidic Craft of the Wise, Connie de Masters, observed the lively marketplace with the quiet demeanor of one who knows. She introduced herself and giggled like a schoolgirl. Her effervescence and joy made me feel as if I were hanging out with my four-year-old best friend. A day or so after the holiday, Connie called and said that she had been told by Spirit to invite me over, because she had things that she needed to tell me about magick. I wondered how I had been singled out.

After that, I drove to Long Beach, California, at least once a week to sit at Connie's knee for one-on-one high-magick instruction. My magickal knowledge increased as I listened while she rocked in an Archie Bunker recliner and shared a wealth of multigenerational witchcraft knowledge. Her magickal kids came and left during our hours-long visits. Some took naps on the couch like loyal bats.

Over the course of three years of private lessons, my mind became a well-oiled tool for manifestation. Yet, I wanted to devote myself to the goddess and be protected in turn. I wanted to choose my freedom and no longer shroud myself in darkness or fear. I wanted something bigger than myself, something grand and all-encompassing to guide me.

As my spiritual teacher, Connie could read me like a book. Finally, on a chilly drizzly day in early February, she held up a white seven-day candle.

"Brigid is the Bright One, the Bride. She is the light in dark times. You must choose to walk the light but know the dark. Brigid will give you the vision of your heart's desire, the comfort when you need it most, the protecting flames of the forge. She will be your sword and the spark of creativity that weaves through you in words."

Connie, who was normally prone to fits of giggles, aflutter with pink light and white bubbles, then summoned her extensive power, which emanated from her in the surging waves of a tsunami. She held up a lighter and flicked the flame to life. "This flame was held to Brigid's sacred flame in Ireland," she said. "Her magick is in this fire." She held the flame to the wick of the white candle and handed it to me. "Brigid's magick is with you now."

As I held this connection to Brigid in my hands, I wept with gratitude. I drove home with the lit candle tucked into a box in the wheel well of the passenger seat. When I got home, I held an incense stick to the candle's flame and, when it sparked to life, I touched the fire to my pilot light so that Brigid's protection would fuel the heat of my family's home, warm our bodies, cook our food, and spread her protection, creativity, and light.

It took nearly fifteen years to manifest my vision of living as a fully liberated witch author. Sometimes germination takes longer than expected. I now live an artist's life, writing or teaching about magick or throwing pottery, in a rural mountain home that I share with my newly beloved man. Recently, we visited the Hill of Tara in County Meath, Ireland. I poured a libation of blackberry cordial at Brigid's sacred well and collected a vial of water to bring home to the altar we keep to Brigid at our wood-burning stove.

Nearly every day, I build a fire in my hearth in dedication to Brigid. She walks beside me. She is the spark in my light; she quenches my blade. And her ever-present cloak covers and protects me.

Kindling the Fire

H. Byron Ballard, adapted from Carmichael

I raise the hearth fire
As Brigid would.
The circle of Bride's protection
On the fire and on the stones and on the household all.

In Brigid's Keeping
Each night and each day, I speak the blessing of Brigid.
I am under the shielding of
Good Brigid each day,
I am under the shielding of
Good Brigid each night.
I am under her keeping, early and late, every dark, every light.
Brigid is my companion,
Brigid is my maker of song,
Brigid is my helping-woman,
My guide, my friend.

Love and Honey-Baked Apples

Cairelle Crow

This recipe reminds me of my grandmother's kitchen and how it always felt so filled with love. Her particular talent was cooking and baking, and she is remembered for the way her food brought our family together to share laughter and good times. These baked apples make a simple and delicious dessert that brings to mind Brigid's sacred bees and her Otherworld orchard. When you prepare this for family, friends, or yourself, your kitchen will be infused with warm scents that evoke feelings of hearth and home. Craft it with love and magic in your heart.

Ingredients
- 4 apples of a size and variety of your choice
- 1 or 2 pinches of ground cinnamon for each apple
- 1 tablespoon of honey for each apple
- 1 tablespoon chopped pecans for each apple (optional)

Preheat the oven to 350° and coat a baking dish with butter or nonstick spray. Wash and core each apple, removing all seeds, then hollow out the inside a little bit more. Leave the apple's bottom intact. Place the apples in the coated baking dish.

Sprinkle the cavity of each apple with one or two pinches of cinnamon, then fill each apple with one tablespoon of honey and one tablespoon of chopped pecans (optional). Cover the baking dish with foil and bake until the apples are tender—1 to 1½ hours, depending on the variety and size of the apples. Serve warm, with love, and a scoop of vanilla ice cream.

Rosemary Drop Biscuits

Kelly Jo Carroll

Rosemary is a versatile herb with a corresponding element of fire, which makes it a perfect ingredient in any recipe to which you want to bring that energy. It's also healing and protective, and it offers clarity. Just as Brigid brings her warmth to the hearth and home, so too does rosemary offer its own kind of comfortable magic. These savory biscuits can be made quickly and are delicious when served with whipped honey butter.

Ingredients

  2 cups all-purpose flour
  1 tablespoon baking powder
  1 to 3 tablespoons of sugar (optional)
  ½ teaspoon salt
  ¼ cup fresh chopped rosemary (1 heaping tablespoon if using dry)
  1 cup of cold whole-fat buttermilk
  8 tablespoons of melted butter

Heat the oven to 450°F. Mix the flour, baking powder, sugar (if using), and salt. In a separate bowl, stir the rosemary and milk together, then add melted butter to the milk. The mixture should turn into small clumps. Pour the milk-and-butter mixture evenly over the dry ingredients and stir just until moistened. Immediately drop by heaping tablespoons onto a lightly greased or parchment-lined baking sheet. Bake for 10–12 minutes or until the edges turn golden brown. Serve warm with whipped honey butter. Enjoy!

Whipped Honey Butter

Laura Louella

I love sweet nectar from the hive. The variety of flavors from different regions around the world are a delight to my taste buds. Honey is a golden elixir that holds wonderful childhood memories for me. One such memory is whipped honey butter. On rare occasions, my babysitter would make this delicious treat and give it to me on a crunchy toasted English muffin. I thought I was in heaven.

I see Brigid in the giving of this wonderful treat. Brigid is the patron saint of dairy farmers. It is said that she gave butter and milk to those in need. One day, Brigid gave away all of her milk and cheese and then prayed for her stores to be replenished. When her mother came to the barn, it was full of milk and cheese again. Brigid loved to share. She is our example of generosity. She shows us that asking for what we need and trusting that it will be provided, even when we can't see how, is possible.

Brigid is also a bee goddess. Celtic lore holds that her bees brought their magical nectar from her apple orchard in the Otherworld. Indeed, the sweet taste of honey is otherworldly. Adding these two delicious treats together is simply a divine treat. I typically freelance in the kitchen, so please feel free to modify this recipe to your liking.

Perhaps as you enjoy your treat, you will thank the goddess Brigid or Saint Brigid for her example of giving—not from her abundance, but rather from her love for her people. Brigid shows us again and again that giving from the heart is as much a blessing for the giver as for the recipient. When I look back and remember how excited I was to receive this gift from my babysitter, I am inspired to give an unexpected gift to the people in my life. In this way, I can carry Brigid into the world.

Ingredients

    4 tablespoons butter, room temperature
    2 tablespoons honey
    Dash of cinnamon (optional)

Place the butter in a bowl and beat it by hand or with an electric mixer until it becomes light and fluffy, then add the desired amount of honey. Taste as you go to get just the right amount of sweetness. Add a dash of cinnamon if you desire.

Toast an English muffin or warm a biscuit. Smear as much of the whipped honey butter on top as you desire and enjoy with a cup of your favorite tea.

Brigit Ale-Woman

Mael Brigde

The opening stanza of this poem is from an 11th century work attributed to Saint Brigit that has been translated by Eugene O'Curry in *MS Materials for Irish History* (Dublin, 1861). The red ale referred to is mentioned in "Broccan's Hymn," from the *Liber Hymnorum*.

I should like a great lake of ale
For the King of kings.
I should like the family of heaven
To be drinking it through time eternal.

Brigit would like to offer
Jesus and his companions
a lovely lake of beer

we laughed when we read that
but listen
this is not some drunken debauch
it is nourishment—renewal—
the barely fermented drink
of daily life

Brigit magnificent provider
will not stand aside
from suffering

at her blessing water is fine beer
the scent of wine rises from it
the thirsty drink in abundance
the sick are healed when they swallow
Brigit's ale

red as rowan berries
it overspills all that would confine it
it is the face of human sustenance
of undenying love

Brigit's ale cannot be contained
by a single goblet
or the cauldron of a whole community

it must break the confines
even of a pool

burst out as a spring-fed lake
whose sun-sliced waters shimmer
like sheets of bronze
on the silent evening plain.

Brigid's Wafers

Mary-Grace Fahrun

When I was eight years old, I spent the summer in Italy. Much of my time was spent at the convent of the Sisters of the Presentation of the Blessed Virgin Mary in the Temple in Ostia, outside of Rome. My father's hometown was in the mountains of Abruzzo and his sister was Mother Superior of the convent. The following is a combination of how I remember these events and how my *Zia Suora* ("Aunt Sister") retold the story at least once a year.

Following morning chores and prayers, we all donned smocks and entered a huge room stocked with art tools and supplies. Eight-year-old me thought I had died and gone to plastic-arts heaven! I was handed gouache paints, a soft paintbrush, and a fresh sheet of poster board. What luxury compared to the terrible dime-store watercolors, plastic-bristle paintbrushes, and flimsy scrapbook paper I was used to. I was instructed to "paint what is in your heart." I sort of remember thinking that I wanted to paint green mountains, but I painted a big black shape that looked nothing like mountains instead. I was so upset that I stopped painting.

A sister came over and asked me what was wrong. I explained what I had intended to paint and that I had thrown what I actually painted into the garbage. I wanted to start over. She smiled and said softly: "That would be wasteful. It is not garbage. Look and see what it is and follow that thread." As I stood back and stared at the wavy black image, my mind told me it looked like the hood worn by Little Red Riding Hood in the storybook my mom had read to me when we were still together. Little Red Riding Hood had black hair and a red hood. That sparked an idea, and I went to work.

When I was done, I had painted a girl with long, fiery red hair peeking out of her black hood. One of the sisters called my aunt over to show her. My aunt, a very stern and stoic woman, said: "*Santa Brigida. Brava.*" I did not know who Santa Brigida (Saint Brigid) was, so I was given a picture book of her story that has, sadly, been lost in the mists of time. That same afternoon, when it was time to bake sweets, my painting inspired the sisters to make *i brigidini* instead.

The recipe I share is the one given to me by my aunt. But I did a little research on my own years ago into the origin of these cookies. They were traditionally made on Saint Brigid's feast day of February 1st in Lamporecchio in the province of Pistoia. Today, they are widely available year-round in Italy and are common treats found at fairs and street festivals. According to one of the most accredited legends, their name derives from the error of a nun of the convent of Santa Brigida in Pistoia. The story goes that a sister mistakenly added eggs and sugar to the usual recipe for the host. Realizing her mistake, she decided to use the dough in a different way in order not to waste it. So she added some aniseed, thus creating the famous sweets devoted to Santa Brigida called *i brigidini*. I have carried her lesson of "transform, don't waste" my entire life.

Twenty years later, my father was diagnosed with terminal brain cancer at the exact same time that I was facing a crisis of faith. I had not been Catholic for almost two decades. I was devouring books on Wicca and witchcraft (these terms were interchangeable in the 1990s), but I still felt disconnected from my source. I was searching and searching, and felt as if the ground had been pulled from under my feet. I remember that one night, out of utter desperation, loneliness, and grief from the inevitable loss of my father, I cried myself to sleep. I do not remember what I dreamt that night, but I do remember the next day as vividly as if it were yesterday.

It was a bright, sunny Sunday morning. I set out for Saint Joseph's Oratory followed by a stop at Mélange Magique, a metaphysical store. There, I looked up and saw a statue I had never noticed before. It was of a woman with fiery red hair dressed in a big black hooded cloak. I asked the store owner who it was, and she said: "The goddess Brigid." At that moment, I heard a voice, either in my ear or in my head. It may just have been my own thoughts, but the words were clear as day: "Your mixture is not a mistake. Look and see what it is and follow that thread." And so, I did. And have been ever since.

That was the moment I began to feel that I was no longer lost. That was the moment I began to feel spiritually supported. The ground became solid beneath my feet once again, and I began to put one foot in front of the other. I did not know where I was going. I was simply "following that thread." And that thread has always led me back to Brigid. Sometimes she is Saint Brigid to me. Sometimes she is the goddess Brigid. Sometimes she is just Mother. At times, she is simply the element of fire. No matter what her guise, she is and has always been with me. Protecting me. Guiding me. Even when I become busy with the day-to-day responsibilities of life and forget to check in with her. She is always there.

I use a pizzelle iron to make these cookies, but I imagine pressing the dough in a tortilla press and baking them a few minutes would give you a similar result. These are best enjoyed freshly made, but can be stored quite some time in an airtight container once they are completely cooled.

Ingredients

  1 extra-large egg
  ½ cup sugar
  2 teaspoons of aniseed (optional)
  Pinch of salt
  Flour, just enough

Start by creaming the eggs, sugar, and pinch of salt. Slowly add flour and aniseed until it reaches the consistency of a rather firm dough (like making fresh pasta). Knead with your hands on a pastry board. When the dough is smooth, shape it into a disk, wrap it in cling wrap, and place it to rest in the refrigerator for one hour.

After the dough has rested, take it out of the refrigerator and shape it into balls the size of a walnut. Place them in the pizzelle iron at a suitable distance from each other and let them cook until golden. If using a tortilla press, press out the dough and place the disks on a nonstick cookie sheet. Bake in a 350°F oven for 5–10 minutes, until golden.

Smooring the Fire

H. Byron Ballard, adapted from Carmichael

Brigid Bright Arrow
To save, to shield, to surround
The hearth, the house, the household,
This eve, this night, oh! This eve, this night, and every night,
Every single night.

Rose's Irish Soda Bread

Kimberly Moore

My Irish great-grandmother, Rose O'Neal, always smelled of lavender and bread. Within minutes of being in her home, you found yourself sitting at the kitchen table while she brewed you a cup of tea or put on coffee, with a big hunk of her soda bread and numerous spreadables laid out before you. And then the real magick of the kitchen began—the gab!

When I smell the delicious scent of this bread now, Rose comes to me in an instant. Enjoy this bread with your own loves and make lots of memories!

Ingredients

  2 cups whole wheat flour
  2 cups all-purpose flour
  ½ teaspoon baking powder
  ½ teaspoon baking soda
  1 teaspoon salt
  1½ teaspoons of honey
  2 cups buttermilk

Preheat the oven to 375°F. Combine the dry ingredients in a bowl. Mix by hand for 3–4 minutes. Make a well in the flour mixture and add the honey and buttermilk to the well. Mix by hand until all the liquid is absorbed. Knead lightly four or five times and form into a slightly oval loaf. Place the loaf on a floured baking tray and lightly dust the top with flour. Using the side of your hand, press an X on top of the loaf. Bake for 50 minutes.

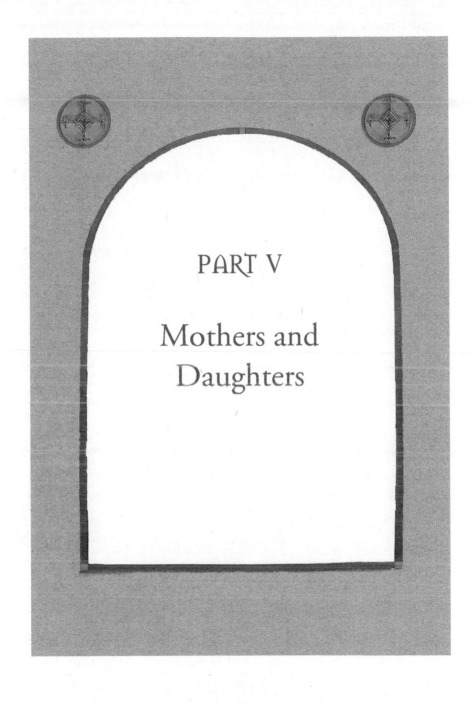

PART V

Mothers and Daughters

The Goddess

Brigid Marie Bennett

My path is not one to find Brigid, for she had already found me long before I found myself.

I was given the name Brigid at birth, named after the reincarnation of the goddess by an Irish Catholic family. Blessings of a handful of ancestral gifts and a Brigid's Cross above my bed bore the markings of my childhood. In my youth, I knew my path was unique, but answers remained in shadow and in secret in the years to follow.

At fifteen, an awakening stirred within my young spirit. I found a peculiar pendant adorned with the goddess Brigid, and this was the spark that ignited the flame illuminating my ever-winding path. It was in that moment that I remembered the call, her call. The dreams began as soon as the pendant was placed on my altar, where it still resides. There was a powerful message within that very first dream: The seed of life is the answer to the problems of the world. As age crept slowly into my youth, so did an understanding of that message and its connection with Brigid.

The years that followed were shrouded in shadow, an era of self-discovery through the darkness. I spent years submerged in a career that overwhelmed every aspect of my life. I could sense Brigid's call as it deepened and persisted through my work as a healer, a nurse. An intricate, handwoven Brigid's Cross that hangs above my oven is evidence of my journey, gifted to me by the daughter of a patient years after he had passed. I'd sat with this patient in his final moments and his daughter, while in Ireland, came upon this small cross in a little shop and felt her father with her in that moment. The small, makeshift paper inscription that came with the cross told the story of Saint Brigid, who had sat with a dying man and woven him a cross from reeds in his final moments. My patient's daughter felt its pull and knew it was meant to find its way to me. Another call from the goddess through another's life.

Motherhood unlocks the deepest parts of our souls. My journey into motherhood began with my son, my first miracle. Within motherhood, I found the courage to own my truth. I found the courage to come out from the shadows. I found the courage to open my shop, which is deeply rooted within my spiritual path as I work side by side with the goddess to create. My courage was rewarded as doors began to open.

I started my journey as a silversmith apprentice. A single sheet of silver transmuted into a Brigid's Cross with only my hands and my tools became my first piece crafted in the metal. Immediately after seeing this piece, a priestess of Brigid extended her hand to me. Three days later, a forgotten anvil buried in time beneath the forge of my late grandfather, a blacksmith, was unearthed and gifted to me. If ever there was a moment of truth and understanding between the goddess and me, that moment was it. It was no longer a call; it was a yell.

As I find myself along my path, I find Brigid, for she found me long before I found myself.

Figure 13. The Fleming Sisters. Josephine Fleming, left, with her sister Elizabeth. The Fleming sisters came to the United States from Tipperary, Ireland. According to family lore, they had passage booked on the *Titanic*, but their mother fell ill and they stayed behind for a few extra days. Josephine is the great-grandmother of Brigid Marle Bennett. Photo from the private collection of Brigid Marie Bennett.

Daughter of Bride

Diane DiPietro

I rise up through the layers of mist to travel to her place
And come upon a mighty woman of surprising grace.
She quickly glances at me, her eyes meet my awestruck gaze.
She wordlessly gestures to me that I am welcome to remain.

I watch as she pulls a piece of forged iron from the fire
And places it upon an anvil to inspect and admire.
I find a seat upon a log and watch the Lady work
And slowly take in the view from my tiny perch.

Her place is a clearing in a deep thick forest, of which I know not the
    name,
Since it is hidden from the view of most, it has no visible path to
    take.
You must search deep inside you, as you come upon it only by fate!
Her wooden cabin emits a cozy glow from the fire lit within it.
The smell of something warm and sweetly simmering tantalizes my
    senses!

I am brought back to myself, seated upon the log,
As the sudden sound of hammering raises me from my fog.
I turn to see the Lady adjust the metal she has wrought.
As I stare in wonder at her forging skills,
She again meets my gaze and shares a smile that gives me chills!

"I am the Goddess Bride," she says, turning her work once more.
"You now belong to me, of that you can be sure."
I feel a glowing warmth of love wash over my entire being.
I know in this moment that I am on a fated journey.

"I am the light in the darkness when you feel most lost.
I am the voice within your heart that helps you find your spark.
I do not promise you your path will need no effort,
But follow me and I will help you be your truest."

"Listen for my voice when you are feeling your most dire.
My wailing at its very core will set your soul on fire!
When you feel lost with no direction in your life,
Listen for my whistle in the darkness, let it guide you back from
    strife!"

"I am she who heals your soul if you'll only let me.
Whether through turmoil or sleepless nights, I will rock you gently.
And when you need to battle against that which is hateful,
I will forge a sword for you to conquer those who are baneful."

"Follow me, be my daughter, let me show you how.
To live a life of joy and confidence, take my hand, *now*!"

Sisters

M. A. Phillips

The state park was lush with early summer's growth and jubilant bird-song—the perfect environment for a baby blessing. Beyond the trees, conversation hummed with anticipation as the Druids prepared. The bard would begin drumming soon, and they would process to their places amid a rousing chorus. They would offer freshly harvested herbs to the bonfire, call out to the gods, and welcome their newest member, baby Oscar.

Dora passed the infant to her husband, Donald, and scurried to greet her sister in the parking lot. As usual, Colleen wore a beautiful dress. The light green fabric flowed over her like the graceful drape of weeping willow fronds at the park entrance. Dora had selected a sky-blue sundress to coordinate with her son's sailboat shirt, and was secretly delighted at how well it complemented her sister's wardrobe.

Their parents hadn't yet arrived, but since Colleen had a part to play in the rite of passage, Dora had suggested that she come earlier to meet with the senior Druid for any last-minute questions.

"It'll be a super-relaxed ritual," Dora promised. "We chant a lot, and we have a specific way of doing things, but we try not to be very stuffy. Nobody will grumble if you don't sing along or make offerings yourself. Oh, and I have something for you."

She dug through her bag and presented a cardboard jewelry box to Colleen. Her sister accepted the gift and Dora prayed to her goddess that Colleen would recall the conversation they had had three weeks before and appreciate what she had found.

The knock had come at precisely one o'clock. Dora hadn't finished folding the laundry, a task she'd ambitiously set out to do during an unexpected lull, but she opened the door with a gracious salutation. She had texted the invitation, after all. Colleen glided in like a cloud and pressed Dora into her angelic white dress.

"Thank you for coming," Dora said and stepped back. She flattened the wrinkles from her nursing T-shirt and hoped the fleck of spit-up wasn't too visible. "Perhaps I'm a little underdressed?"

Colleen waved a hand and hung her matching purse on one of the four chairs at the kitchen table. "Oh, gosh, don't fuss. I have a meeting with some ladies from church after this. We're finalizing our plans for the summer bake sale. I can't decide if I should do cupcakes or chocolate chip cookies. Anyway, if I had a newborn, I'd go for relaxed too! Speaking of that, where is my adorable nephew?"

Bobbing her head for her sibling to follow, Dora padded toward the nursery. On the way, they passed a watercolor of a divine woman with swirling, red hair. A bookshelf below housed a collection of stones, candles, and ceramic bowls. Despite the disarray elsewhere, Dora managed to replace the vase of flowers and dust this bookshelf once a week.

"Is that . . . a skull?" Colleen asked, pausing before the altar.

Dora looked over her shoulder and grinned. "A skull-shaped rose quartz, but yeah. Pretty, right?"

"I was going to say 'creepy,' but to each their own, I guess."

"I'd had my eye on it for months, and Donald surprised me when we came home with Oscar. I like to think it represents my ancestral mothers looking out for me," Dora explained, her voice dropping to a whisper as she entered Oscar's room. "He usually wakes up after I move him to his crib. I can't believe he's napped so long!"

Any discomfort from the skull figure faded in the aura of the snoozing baby. A ring of soft forest animals hung from a mobile to guard their prince. Oscar's tiny limbs splayed out without any worries as his belly, full of milk, rose and fell rhythmically.

Colleen beamed and touched the cross over her chest. "He's so precious."

Dora gestured back to the kitchen. "C'mon. I want to talk to you about something while I can. He's bound to wake up soon, and you'll get your cuddles then."

She prepared a mug of coffee for Colleen and a cup of lactation tea for herself. Before serving, Dora said a silent prayer to Brigid: "Blessed lady, protector of mothers and children, please help me nurture my son. Wrap your calming blanket around my sister so she can be part of our celebration. So be it."

Colleen inhaled the rich aroma from her cup. "Ahh! I needed this pick-me-up. So, what's new? It's unusual for you to ask me for favors or advice. This must be huge."

Dora placed a tray of scones on the table and took a seat. "Yeah, well . . . This isn't something I can ask anyone else."

Her sister raised an eyebrow, but her skepticism vanished momentarily when she bit into a scone. "These taste just like Grandma's!"

"Good! I found the recipe when I helped mom organize all her things. There was a big trunk of stuff none of us knew about."

Colleen scrunched her lips and pretended to examine one of her sister's prolific pothos plants. Grandma had moved beyond the veil three months earlier, and Colleen avoided the topic as much as possible.

"You don't need to feel guilty," Dora said and patted her hand. "I realize death makes you uneasy, and I certainly won't judge you for that. Anyway, I asked you here because I was wondering if you would be Oscar's godmother?"

Colleen gaped at her. "Wait, are you actually baptizing him?"

"No! No. But that is the best description for the job. Donald and I are organizing a baby-blessing ceremony with our Druid grove. And we hope you'll be there and agree to watch over Oscar."

"Ah." Colleen stared into the dark liquid in her mug. "Are Mom and Dad going?"

"I haven't talked to them yet, but I'm sure they'll be more inclined to come if you're there too. Look, I understand what I do and believe aren't your thing. I'm not trying to convert you. I just want to share this important day with you and know that you'll take care of Oscar should something happen to Donald and me, gods forbid."

Silence hovered in the air, like smoke from a ritual bonfire. Colleen once more gripped her necklace, and her older sister did the same. Dora's bore a three-legged spiral; Colleen's a crucifix.

"Heaven forbid anything ever happens to you, but if it did, you know I'd care for Oscar as if he were my own. I love him to bits! But I'm not sure I could raise him the way you intend to. No offense."

Dora rolled her eyes. "I'm not asking you for that; only that you make sure my child doesn't starve! Now, let's leave the morbid hypotheticals alone and focus on what is happening in the near future."

"The—what did you call it?—baby blessing?"

"Yes. Essentially, we'll formally introduce Oscar to our grove and spirit allies. We'll pray for protection and his happiness as he grows. Along with coming to witness the rite, I simply ask that you hold him and promise to be there for him through his life."

Colleen's shoulders bounced. "Easy peasy. I can handle that." She took another bite of her scone.

Dora smiled and winced at the same time.

"What's that look for?" Colleen asked.

A manila folder waited beside Dora. She opened it now and handed a sheet of paper to her sister. "I highlighted your part in yellow."

"Wait. There's a script?"

Dora chewed her own scone while Colleen scanned the liturgy. "Not exactly. The head Druid will recite that, and then you'll repeat. Like you said. Easy peasy."

"'Swear by land, sea, and sky?' Dora, this is the sort of stuff I can't get into."

"You'd only make a promise to Oscar. When I discussed this with the grove, I was emphatic about that. No other spirits. No other gods. Just you making an oath to your nephew and us. I wanted to compromise so you'd be comfortable. The wording just matches the symbolism throughout."

"I'm not sure I'll ever be entirely comfortable going to one of your rituals."

"Never mind." Dora carried the dish of scones to the cupboard along with her cup, but it toppled over, spilling its now lukewarm contents across the counter. "Shoot!"

Colleen jumped up, but Dora was efficient, and perhaps the tension would have dissipated in that moment of clumsiness if it hadn't been for the whimpers coming from down the hall. Their volume climbed into a wail, so Dora dashed to the nursery.

Reluctant to leave without a proper farewell, Colleen loitered in the kitchen. Her sister's altar drew her like a forbidden book at the library. A shot glass held the remnants of this morning's tea, given to an unknown being Dora revered. Colleen glanced at the woman depicted above the shelves while Dora shushed Oscar in the distance. The gentle melody of a lullaby floated into the room.

They appeared a moment later. Dressed in a green onesie, Oscar nuzzled against Dora while she rocked from side to side. She stroked his dark tufts of hair and met her sister's gaze.

"Sorry for the wait. Little Oscar needed a new diaper. Didn't you?" She kissed her son's head. "Would you like to hold him?"

They maneuvered the baby from one to the other and, while Oscar whined for his mother at first, he soon snuggled against his aunt.

"He's getting so big already!"

"Yeah, I think he takes after his father. I bet Oscar will be as tall as he is someday. Like an oak tree!" Dora leaned against the wall facing her altar. "I'm sorry for making you uncomfortable. I tried to find a way to include you, but I guess the very act of attending one of my grove's rites would make you anxious."

Colleen traced her nephew's round cheeks as he studied her features. She made a clicking noise with her tongue and earned an intrigued coo. "He's so cute! How can I say no to this sweet face?"

"Wait," Dora said, squinting at her sister. "Does this mean you'll come to the baby blessing?"

Oscar reached toward the sound of his mother's voice, so Colleen returned him.

"Yes. I'll do it. No matter your religion, I'm still your sister and his aunt."

The scent of flowers from the garden wafted in through an open window. A shaft of sunlight settled over the altar, and the holy woman in the frame sparkled as loops of gold leaf through her hair and across her emerald kirtle were illuminated.

After fetching her mug, Colleen rejoined Dora and Oscar in the sunbeam. "Who is that in the picture?"

Dora's lips stretched like petals lengthening in summer's radiance. "That's Brigid. A grove mate painted her for me as a baby-shower gift."

"A goddess then?"

"Yes." Dora nodded and shifted her son so that they faced the image. "And a saint."

Colleen moved closer. "What do you mean?"

"She's both. Well, depending on whom you ask." Dora adjusted Oscar and ordered her words. "Some say Saint Brigid was Mary's midwife."

Colleen wrinkled her brows. "Oh yeah?"

Her sister shrugged. "It's folklore, so you need to think of it differently. Saint Brigid's a healer, and beloved around Ireland. Her feast day just happens to occur on the same day as that of a pre-Christian goddess who shares her name. So their lore weaves together like the blanket draped over her, and it can be difficult to spot where the deity ends and the saint begins." Dora's eyes swept toward Colleen. "Even though I left Catholicism, I find great comfort in that. Brigid aided me with healing a lot of old wounds and insecurities—to the point where, should you ever ask me to attend a wedding or baptism at your church, I would be able to go without hesitation. I'm sure I'd be a bit awkward, but I would seek Brigid's familiar warmth. Perhaps she can help you do the same at the baby blessing."

Colleen opened the dainty box Dora had handed her and found a silver medallion within. The metal oval featured a woman in a robe and wimple. She held a staff in one hand and an equal-armed cross in the other.

"Saint Brigid of Ireland," Colleen read the engraved name and gasped. "Where did you find this? Don't tell me you actually went into a Catholic gift store."

Dora giggled. "Are you worried I'd burst into flame? No, I found it among Grandma's things, and Mom let me take it. Initially, I was drawn to it because of my goddess. Honestly, I think Grandma would want me to give it to you. Goddess or saint, Brigid can help us understand and support one another, since she walks with many different people."

Though her eyes watered, Dora helped her sister with the clasp. When Colleen turned around, tears gathered at her lashes.

"Thank you so much! This is such an amazing heirloom. Do you think it came with Grandma from Ireland?"

"Perhaps. In honor of the occasion, I'm going to make an offering of Grandma's scones to her and Brigid. But don't worry—I made plenty more for the potluck afterward! Are you ready to come to your first-ever Druid ritual?" Dora asked, smirking.

Colleen caressed the necklace her grandmother had left behind. The sisters walked beside one another below an arch of maple trees, and it seemed that a third woman strode between them and held their hands.

Figure 14. With her characteristic cross, this Brigid of Healing watches over the entranceway to the artist's home, as Brigid's Crosses traditionally do over the doors to others' homes. She was painted as part of a series following a trip to Ireland and marks the absolute balance point when the Divine Feminine changed over from goddess to saint and continued its expression. Art by Nic Phillips.

Four Archetypal Poems

Marion Brigantia van Eupen

Maiden Bridie

Bridie bright
Maiden of Light
Bridie, young and pure
You who carry the innocence
of my magical child,
who knows where to find the Unicorn,
in the wild forests of my life.
You who are the fire of healing
within us, lighting up the dark places
in my memory to be held in your love.
You who are the ignition of
the flame of inspiration,
showing new ways of being.
I see You breaking through
the frozen earth as snowdrops,
so fragile and still so resilient.
I hear your presence
in every breath,
singing in the Springtime,
as the light returns.
I feel You touching me
with your white rod
stirring the source of my potential,
meeting me in You,
Maiden Bridie,
I see myself
True.

Lover Bridie

I follow You
to the wide-open places,
running through fields of flowers
dancing in the fiery sunlight
celebrating the passion
that drives me,
embracing the love that lifts
me high above the ordinary.
I follow the traces of your serpent,
ever changing, twisting, turning,
Kundalini energy rising from the earth.
Inviting me to open all my senses,
to hear, to see, touch and smell
intensely, the aliveness of all of nature.
As I merge with You,
beloved of my heart
closer than my heartbeat
drumming the rhythm of wild ecstasy.
My blood spiraling freely
from the source of my being,
meeting me in You,
Lover Bride,
I feel myself
Loved.

Mother Bridget

I follow You,
to the fertile lands,
where my steps
synchronize with the resounding
rhythm of your heartbeat.
The place of creation,
where You show me how to allow
trust to grow into abundance.
You, who are the waving fields

of golden grain at harvest time;
the flowing light of your cosmic cow;
nourishment for my soul.
You invite me into your loving embrace
which unlocks all the lost places inside:
the times that I could not find You
when I did not know of You.
There, You light your hearth fire,
hospitable and warm
and still I linger on the threshold.
There, You feed me
from Your healing cauldron,
the true medicine that comes
from unconditional love
and still I wonder if I am deserving.
Here You touch my heart
softly and tenderly;
meeting me in You,
Mother Bridget,
I welcome myself
Home.

Crone Brighid

I follow You to the liminal places,
between space and time,
following the footprints
of your wise white wolf
into the unknown.
Here You teach me to howl,
to keen for all that I've lost,
offering You my sadness and despair.
In return You offer me a key
which opens the gateway,
into your Smithy.
Here your forge fires
burn strong and bright,

shining your light deep inside
touching the darkest places within me;
melting away all the dross,
all that is not real or not mine to carry.
With every echoing beat of my heart,
the lead turns to gold,
pain transformed to peace
anger transformed to love
fear transformed in trust.
I emerge from your waters,
the source of my own
ancient knowledge,
meeting me in You,
Crone Brighid;
I know myself
Whole.

Figure 15. *Brigantia*, protector goddess and healer. Depicted with the sacred flame and a Brigid's Cross. Painting by Marion Brigantia van Eupen.

Great-Granddaughter of the Well

Yeshe Matthews

I never meant to go to Ireland. I mean, I had a vague idea that one day I might have a chance to kiss the Blarney Stone, and I had been told as a child that, on my mother's father's side, our family was a nebulous blend of "Irish-German," and that we might have somehow been associated with an "Irish mafia" in New York City back in the day. But on the whole, my Irish heritage was lost amid the rowdy, boisterous, first-generation-ness of my Polish and French-Canadian lineages. I grew up eating cabbage and potatoes, but they were boiled with kielbasa, not corned beef. My grandmother spoke French to me as a child, taught me about proper table manners according to Emily Post, and played a mean game of Crazy Eights. It was hardly as if I had a traditional upbringing as a great-granddaughter of Éire. So imagine my surprise, when, one wintry day in January 1999, I found myself buying a plane ticket from New York City to Dublin.

It was Margo's idea to go to Ireland. Margo was my grad school roommate. She had grown up in a privileged family and had already traveled extensively by the time she was in her early twenties. I had been raised by teachers, and we had scrimped and struggled through most of my life, at one point living as a family of three on $4,000 a year. I had only been on an airplane once in my life—a thirty-minute flight from Buffalo to Albany that was considered an extravagant birthday gift from my parents, who knew how desperately I wanted to experience a plane ride. For the record, I was airsick the whole time and threw up immediately upon landing. But I flew! I flew!

Margo was determined, and she made it seem so simple. All we had to do was buy the plane tickets, book a rental car, and then find hostels and BnBs where we could stay along the way. We could set our own agenda. We could do whatever we wanted. It didn't have to be expensive, and we could create a lifetime of memories, she said. We wanted to be in Dublin for Saint Patrick's Day, but after that, she didn't have any clear itinerary.

But I did. I didn't know what Ireland might hold for me, except for one thing—the Cathedral of Saint Brigid in Kildare. Something about Brigid the saint called to me, and I knew in my heart of hearts that I just had to visit it. But I knew little to nothing of Brigid the goddess.

The time between planning the trip and leaving seemed to go by in a flash. Suddenly, I found myself boarding an Aer Lingus flight in New York with a cheap suitcase, a pocket full of Dramamine, and some cash I had exchanged at an abysmal rate at an airport kiosk. Margo had all of the smoothness of an experienced traveler, complete with a cute little neck pillow, a satin eye mask, and slippers just for the plane and her comfortable first-class flight. I was rough around the edges and nervous, without any idea of what to expect as I traveled on a red-eye in economy.

When I landed and picked up my luggage, I had about eight hours to kill before Margo arrived and we could check into our hostel. I was so tired from flying all night that I could barely keep my eyes open. I managed to find a bus that took me from the airport into Dublin and from there I stumbled into the National Gallery, which opened bright and early. I checked my luggage and coat, and wandered bleary-eyed through the museum, admiring images by artists whose names I'd never heard before. I found a room where there were big, devotional paintings of the Virgin Mary. In the middle of the room was a kneeling bench so that people could pray before the images. Gratefully, I knelt down, buried my face in my hands, whispered a thank-you to the Virgin, and promptly fell asleep.

After my power nap in the National Gallery, I felt somewhat refreshed. I found a cafe and had a little pot of tea, feeling worldly and sophisticated as I watched the cars go by and listened to the accents all around me. Margo and I met up when she landed and we headed to our hostel. We planned to spend a few days in and around Dublin, visiting local spots of interest before hitting the road to as-yet-unknown destinations.

At Kilmainham Gaol, my blood boiled to learn of the injustice and inhumanity visited upon political prisoners; at the Temple Bar, my teen obsession with Sinead O'Connor was fulfilled by walking where she used to work as a waitress; and just north of the city, the sacred cavern at Newgrange offered the humbling presence of ancestral dreams and a frisson of excitement as a simulated sunrise filled the chamber with light. I'll never forget watching the parade through the streets of Dublin on Saint Patrick's Day. And there were some big surprises in that parade!

Because many Irish dignitaries actually left Ireland to celebrate Saint Patrick's Day in other places around the world, the parade was full of people from—well, everywhere else. There were midwesterners from the Ancient Order of Hibernians. There were a few different groups of Scotsmen in kilts playing bagpipes. There were Brazilian Capoeiristas and a host of other non-Irish folks who were just happy to be in the parade. Looking back, it was a little bit weird and disjointed, but I was uncritically happy to be there. It felt exotic, novel, and magical to me. Little did I know that the magic was just beginning.

When we left Dublin, we ventured northwest, skirting Northern Ireland and ending up in County Donegal for several days. Donegal was my favorite—so green, fresh, and relaxing. There was a spot called the Bloody Foreland that I had found mentioned in an Irish travel guide, where red granite cliffs rise out of the blue-grey sea. When the sun sets, the red stone takes on a vivid hue. This was not a battle site or a monument to violence, but rather a celebration of the rich, red blood of Mother Earth. I wanted to go. This was before cell phones were common and before GPS could lead you almost anywhere. So Margo and I hopped into our rental car and just started driving vaguely in the direction of the coast.

At a certain point along the way, something came over me and I began to have a very strong sense that I knew, somehow, the way to our destination. We drove and drove, with me navigating intuitively, and arrived there exactly at sunset. We pulled over to ask a little boy who was playing a lonely game of ball on the dirt road if he could direct us to the Bloody Foreland. The bemused answer came: "You're on it!" Just a hundred feet more and we were at the edge of the world. It was a beautiful moment, seeing the rusty color of the stone bathed in the cooling evening sun. Those photos are long since lost, although I may someday find them in my mother's basement. But the memory remains indelible.

After the beauty of Donegal, we enjoyed the art and culture of Galway and then dove into more countryside exploration, visiting castle ruins, small churches, and a host of pubs where we tried in vain to meet cute guys. We were used to the bold, assertive mating rituals of young American men, but Irish fellows were not interested in our flirting. So we mostly spent our time hanging out with each other, chatting with the hosts at the hostels and BnBs where we stayed, studying our guidebooks, and reading the plaques and signs of the places where we went exploring.

The entire time we were wending our way through the Irish country-side, I kept one goal in mind—to get to Kildare and see Brigid's cathedral. The day before we were due back in Dublin to fly home, we drove across Ireland from west to east, and I insisted that we stop in Kildare along the way, even though it was not strictly on our route. Margo seemed bored and frustrated by my insistence that we visit yet another big, old church. She seemed almost relieved when we found ourselves staring at a huge, locked gate in Kildare bearing a sign declaring that the church was closed until April. But I was crushed. The view of the edifice took my breath away, and I felt that I just had to find a way in. How would I manage it?

Just as when I had sensed my way to the Bloody Foreland, I felt an intuitive stirring arise within me. To Margo's surprise, I turned abruptly and marched down the street, scoping out the row of houses that lined the way up to the cathedral gate. One of the houses pulled at me strongly, so, without thinking twice, I walked up to the door and knocked. A petite, surprised, middle-aged woman appeared at the door. "Yes?" she queried.

"I'm here from very far away, from America," I began hesitantly. "I'm on a trip with my friend and, well, I really wanted to see Brigid's cathedral. But now it's closed and I don't know when or if I will ever get to come back here, and I really, really want to go inside and just have a look at it. Do you have any idea if it would be possible to find the caretaker or someone who could let us inside?"

My words came out in a jumble, awkwardly, and I could hardly believe I was hearing myself say them. The lady at the door reached back behind her with a smile and brought forth a big ring of antique keys, saying kindly: "Well, you're in luck. You've found her."

Brigid's emissary—for I now believe that this woman was an ema-nation of Brigid herself—took us on a spectacular private tour of the cathedral, showing us the obvious and hidden histories of the place. Her experience of the space was so intimate and personal, and her stories about everything from the furniture to the stone carvings to the crypts revealed a deep affection for the space. She paused with us under a stained glass window to discuss the legend of Pope Joan. She commanded us (and we did it!) to crawl underneath the crypt of Bishop Wellesley to see the *Sheela Na Gig*, a figurative carving of a naked woman with an exaggerated vulva, found throughout most of Europe. Finally, she took us out into the fire temple and, in the gloaming evening light, she told us the deeper story of Kildare—*Cill Dara*, the land of the oaks. She explained how this area was an ancient site where Druids may have held ceremonies, where Pagan priestesses of the goddess Brigid tended a perpetual flame. Later, an order of nuns inhabited the site, where the magic of the ancestors was still believed, witnessed, and felt.

As she spoke, I felt the caretaker's words weaving a spell around me. From the time I was thirteen, I had identified as a witch, had read books by Raymond Buckland, Scott Cunningham, and Margot Adler. I loved to burn candles and incense. But I was inexperienced. Having been raised in a strict Catholic home, I had not yet really grasped the concept of polytheism. That evening on the grounds of Brigid's cathedral, I was struck by the caretaker's words like an oak tree by lightning.

All of a sudden, I understood that the magic I had always believed *might* be real, could actually *become* real. It was in the air all around us, like electricity. I realized that the stories of magic I had read and heard were not just myths and legends; they were the experiences of people just like me who *believed*. And there was a goddess involved, not just a saint. Not just a female relegated to half citizenship in the land of the holy, but an actual living goddess! When Brigid's emissary laughingly mentioned that men didn't want to enter Brigid's holy fire temple for fear of losing their virility, I was so struck by the power of that concept that I almost fainted.

My mind was awhirl as we gratefully thanked our hostess and found our way back to the car, with the advice that we hurry to see Brigid's well before dark. We zoomed our way to the Japanese Garden and found the older well of Brigid, not the one that tourists usually find. This well is tucked away, unmarked, without much fanfare. But its tremendous life force, its potency, and its history are intact.

Standing there by the sacred well, I was deeply moved by the sudden realization that Brigid actually *wanted* me to find her. That she had arranged all of this for me. That, despite my ignorance and cultural distance from my Irish heritage, I was still a great-granddaughter of Éire. That

I would never be turned away when I sought her magic with an open and respectful heart. In a flash of my mind's eye, I saw a future unfolding. Ten years later, in 2006, I actualized that vision when I opened my shop, The Sacred Well, in Berkeley.

I keep a shrine to Brigid to this day. She has never been far from me in all of my journeys, in my times of joy and sorrow, in my business and in my home. For some, she is the forge; for some, she is the bard. For me, she is like the water from her own well—silent, peaceful, ever-upwelling, and necessary to life. I don't make a lot of noise about my work with Brigid. It's private and personal. But she is always there, always quenching me when I am thirsty for magic and divine intercession.

Battle Call

J. Ellen Cooper

Brigid, so burns your flame of light
as mine within my core
please, lend me that bejeweled shield
mistake not: this is war
help me to maintain my truth,
stand strong,
be your eyes mine
when I walk into that room,
flanked by the warriors of time.
from you I ask: please, tend my fire
stoke it as I fight,
get up, live through this every day.
please, keep our flame alight

Diana, take your aim
steady that chert arrowpoint
upon the eye of the storm
and with your strength in my forearms we will pin destiny in form
from you, I beg, keep intention aimed:
I will leave this charred landscape and enter back into lush
we will leave, yes, strong and soon,
all three woven
plaited tight,
I will not leave without my children

Andraste, your raven wings spread far
across this torched land
and I shall release the energies
freeing hares by word,
by hand.

victory soar over my landscape
as every oak stands tall
and all the grasses on the sinuous hills
are part of the vigilante call
this grove towers with truth and love,
but now we are at war,
a usual weather of peace,
but in righteousness we battle
so let this soul soar free
please, bring your sway of victory
and in the celebration that follows the fight
we will dance for freedom, love, forgiveness, strength, and light

Hathor, rain down upon us
let down from the Milky Way
that the landscape may be nourished
healthy, strong for battle day

Bast, weave in the rhythm
to keep the land a-hum
with vibrations of goodness and freedom
and all our bodies will dance as one

Magdalene, add jive to that rhythm
keep beat for the womanly wiles
accused but true in word; in self
as Kali arranges the tiles

Figure 16. Brigid's quilts. Stitched by the author, these quilts are not fancy, but they are treasured possessions in her home. The love and care stitched into each quilt holds memories; the carefully saved swatches of fabric, when sewn together, tell their own stories of lives lived. The quilted bee pillow represents the author's love for the gathering of family. Photo by Laura Louella.

The Circle

Laura Louella

The circle is cast, all the women are present and ready to begin their ritual of preparing and sharing. They have traveled from near and far, from neighboring farms and homes, on their carts and buggies, for their special day. They have packed a lunch to spread and share; the sweet tea is ready. Every woman has waited for this day for months. The anticipation of this special moment can be felt in the air!

All year, each woman has been saving little scraps of fabric. Every piece of clothing that has been outgrown goes into the quilting pile. Torn clothing that can't be repaired or that has a stubborn stain that can't be removed will be used in the quilt as well. Each piece of precious fabric will be cut into an appropriate size or shape and lovingly sewn together. They wasted nothing in their attempt to be ready for the cold winter months.

These quilts were called utility quilts. They were not fancy, but they were treasured possessions in each home. There was love, care, and thoughtfulness stitched into each quilt top. Quilts held memories for these families; the swatches of fabric told their own stories. When they were sewn together, they morphed into masterpieces of lives lived.

All of the materials have been gathered—the backing, which was usually tea-stained feed or tobacco sacks, and the middle, which was either cotton that was picked by my grandma and her brothers or an old blanket that was too tattered to use alone. This quilt would be a reflection of the determination of women who knew what their families needed to survive.

Once the quilt top was prepared, the three layers were stretched across the frame, taut and ready to receive the thread. Chairs were placed around the frame. Finally, after so much preparation and waiting, the women came to sit around the frame and weave magic with their needles and thread. This was their time to commune with one another, to share the highs and lows of the year. To create magic with their tools and skills. They sewed their intentions of a warmer future into the quilt. Each stitch was a hope, a dream, a prayer.

If you look closely, you will see her there, full of her own delight at being invited to join the circle. She sits under the quilters' frame, all big eyes and listening ears. A little girl, Louise, who will one day, in the distant future, become my grandma.

Louise threaded the needles and, when the occasion arose, removed inadvertent knots. She helped those whose vision had begun to fade. She was the worker bee, learning from the queens. This was her threshold— one foot in her childhood, one foot in her becoming. This liminal space filled her with wonder and gave her a glimpse of her future.

Louise loved the stories she heard under the frame. She was an impressionable little girl as she sat and learned the ways of all who came before her in that circle of women. Sometimes they forgot she was there and told stories that would not be told had they remembered her presence. This was their place to let go, to find comfort and reassurance. She learned of marriages and babies; she heard of illness and death. Grandma told me that she let the words soak in and realized that, to endure and thrive, she must be resilient, never giving in when adversity strikes. She was being initiated into what women face, sometimes alone. But she also learned that she could gather in a safe circle of wise women and find comfort. Grandma drew on this well of ancestral knowledge throughout her life.

Louise watched as old hands pulled the thread, creating designs in the quilts. Magically, they laid beauty down in stitches—a beauty that previously was not there. Those whose vision had faded but whose minds were sharp knew how to create this beauty through habit. Louise sat in this circle of family and friends preparing, always preparing. Those ladies wove a story with their words. They buzzed with the excitement of telling of times long ago and the happenings that had brought them to the present.

I dare say it was so much more than quilting. In the circle, Grandma learned about her own grandmother, whom she loved dearly, and of all the grandmothers and aunts who had come before. She was shaped under the quilters' frame on a big front porch in rural Louisiana. In her life, she often found comfort reminiscing and drinking deeply from this sacred time with her matriarchal line.

At the quilting bee, Louise was the child preparing to become my mom's mother. She began cherishing and respecting what it had taken for her family to travel to and through America. What they had left behind and what they had brought with them were all treasures that my grandma gathered under the quilters' frame. Her heart swelled with the information she gleaned, and it was stitched into her heart.

And right in the middle of all this is Brigid, standing with these ancestors down through the generations. She traveled here with them from Ireland, Scotland, and England. She never left their side. Brigid is the goddess/saint of her people. She cares for them in all aspects of life. As they traveled over the Atlantic Ocean, I know she was holding their hands, comforting them in their time of unspeakable uncertainty. She gave them a bridge to the past and hope for the future. Brigid is the flame that kept them going when life felt too hard. They looked to her each morning as the sun rose. She was their constant companion, the warrioress who encouraged them to stand for what was theirs. When these ancestors came here and life was not what they expected, Brigid caused them to stand strong and carry on.

The Lady of the Well nourished them with love and provided them with fortitude and an assured sense of confidence. When my family wondered where the next meal would come from or how the house that had burned down would ever be replaced, Brigid's waters were the balm that soothed their souls. She inspired dreams to guide them, even when fear could have stopped them in their tracks. She wrapped her cloak around their shoulders and loved them.

Brigid taught my grandma that the sun rises every morning and, in the dawn, if we look and listen, we will see the spark, the flame—the goddess and saint who traveled here with my family into the unknowns of America.

At the exact right time, my dear and loving grandma began passing the wisdom she had gathered down to me. She taught me to value family, to honor those to whom I am connected by bone and by marrow, to learn from those whose blood pulses through me. My ancestors are the golden thread that leads me back to those who came before me, and now I take them into the future. The lineage continues.

And I will share with my granddaughter the knowledge that we come from a strong thread of women who loved deeply, had integrity, were courageous, and lived creatively. Every one of my grandmothers back through time experienced hardship. But they faced forward and carried on. They trusted and did not fight the winds of change. Rather they accepted their challenges with open hearts and bravery. Each of them is here with me now, watching over me, correcting me, and directing my path. The flame that led them continues to lead me.

Now, I am the family quilter. I don't have the same challenges my ancestors had in procuring the materials I need to create my quilting magic. But, when I pick up a needle and thread, I am carried back to a distant past, a time when my people gathered to stitch a spell. I hear their whispers and laughter; I sense their tears and frustrations. Still, I know that their love is present for me. In turn, I love them all for their unique contributions to my life. Little bits of each of these women who helped form Louise into my grandmother have also made me into the daughter, mother, Lally, woman I am today!

All of these generations of women are like the three-ply thread used in quilting. We are wound in a circular fashion, bound through time, the separate-yet-connected parts of a whole. We are stitched together like the edges of a quilt. Around the edge of a quilt, there is a continuous strip of fabric, folded and stitched into place, holding the quilt together and making the three parts one. Binding is exactly what happened when these ancestors of mine sat around the quilting frame. They stitched together their love for each other and their families into a future granddaughter who now binds them into her own quilts. We are three strands inextricably woven together, carrying our legacy. We are held tight with the threads that draw us close and keep us united. And this binding protects what is most valuable to our family—love.

We are united as family through the long line that winds back in time to the first mother who picked up needle and thread. Brigid is the Exalted One, keeper of the flame, inspired creator of beautiful things. Her gift to my family is the trinity of transformation, inspiration, and creativity. She brings us together—past, present, and future. Because of these diligent sewing women, this quilting ritual has been stitched into my heart. This is our true and treasured family heirloom. It continues to be passed down to each new generation. Faith, knowledge, and love support us in all ways.

The circle has enlarged and continues unbroken.

Figure 17. Jane Victoria Bridwell Kilpatrick. Photo of the author's great-great grand-mother, the hostess of the quilting circle held on her porch in Louisiana. Photo from the private collection of Laura Louella.

Daughter of Bridget

Mary Tidbury

I am the daughter of the green isle, of the holy thorn, of the deep
   well.
I am the daughter of the swift running boat, of the silver fish, of the
   shining wave.
I am the daughter of the sweet white milk, of the amber honey, of
   the wheaten bread.
I am the daughter of oak, hazel, and yew.
I am the daughter of strong mothers, the mother of strong daughters;
I am the daughter of Bridget.

I've Forgotten the Bhrat

H. Byron Ballard

It is Imbolc and there is still much to do. With one eye, I am following the weather patterns out West and wondering how fast that system is moving. With another eye, I am reviewing the Mother Grove Imbolc ritual for Saturday night. But my third eye is set in the past, in the circle of women who came together for a daylong retreat with holy Brigid.

First, there was soup and bread in the kitchen, holding its richness and nourishment for us. Then there was a small altar set squatly in the snow. And there was a bowl of fire—bright, warm, alive in the center of the circle of women.

We were sitting close together, compressed in the courtyard circle. We shared bits about ourselves and, by noon, we had cried together, laughed together, contemplated the mystery of mothers and daughters together. Because maternal issues loom so large in the culture that holds us, it invited us to create an alternate motherline that led us straight back to Brigid.

We practiced our healing and our dancing. We wandered in the wood and we listened to the voices both inside and out. There was soup and good bread around the fire as well, and fruit and cookies, too.

The time in the wood was mostly silent. A hawk stooped as the journey began, and the young crone held on to the beloved elder crone for dear life.

By the time the soup was finished, we were a tribe of women, a village of sisters. We ended our time together with smoored candles of Brigid's sacred flame and a simple ritual of yarn that wove us wrist-to-wrist into a vessel of magic and healing.

Inspiration. Transformation. Healing. Fire.

I have to set out the Bride's bed tonight and leave her some of the very best whisky in the house. I do this in love, and also in gratitude for her goodness, her presence.

Last night, I had come off a very busy weekend and had a car full of stuff to unload from the retreat. Sundown came and I realized that, not only had I not put out the bhrat, but it was still somewhere in the full car. I was too tired to go out and find it.

Today, I unloaded the car and put everything away. And as I sit here, I have an image of the bhrat setting in the solarium, waiting to be placed on the wet Appalachian soil of my side yard.

Honestly, I won't forget it again. As soon as I've posted this, I'll take it out.

But for this moment, my eyes are in the past, considering the power and beauty of these women who are forged in fire, whose souls sharpen steel, who will never again be vanquished. With such an army of glorious and entwined women, what could be accomplished in these Tower Times, in this old and tired world?

Crone Time

Donna Gerrard

Crow wing feathery blackness wraps the year
Bony fingers grasping
Drawing us deeper, deeper to hibernation cave
Thicker and thicker velvety blackness
Dark sightless eyes
Tongues of fire flame licking the deep dark
Glinting off pregnant cauldron roundness
Boiling the bones of the year
Keening the sun to its death
Tolling its passing with the sharp bell hammer-strike
Dead
Boiled
Burnt
Passed
Ashen
Waiting
A seed in the cold dark frozen earth
Potential
For what comes.

Tending the Flame

Annie Russell

The sun had not yet risen above the horizon, let alone penetrated the deep gray of the pines, as the woman hurried along the path that would bring her to the steep stairs leading down to the beach and the open expanse of Lake Michigan. The spring wind blew gently, but with a chill that cut through the wool sweater and down jacket she had donned for this annual pilgrimage. Daffodils and tulips may herald springtime in other areas of the United States, but in this remote hamlet of northern Michigan, spring brought frozen mud and a lighter shade of gray to the afternoon skies. Hummocks of dirty snow still held fast along the roads, but deep within the pine forest, the ground was more slushy than snowy. The wind coming off the massive inland sea ahead of her was cold and unforgiving.

Hoisting the basket higher onto her hip, she made her way carefully down the steep stairs—stairs carved decades ago from fallen pines and worn smooth and slippery with time and the elements that the lake threw at the forest day after day, month after month, year after year. The heavy boots, made for expeditions like this, gripped the rustic steps, keeping her from falling head over heels down to the bottom, where the sand still held a frozen crust of water, pebbles, and pine boughs.

The sun began to creep through the trees, casting flickering shadows that danced and swayed as she moved ahead, like excited children running ahead to see what lay around the next turn. A gull cried overhead, lending its laughter to the dancing shadows and the busy waves as the woman broke free of the treacherous steps and the dark pine forest. She sucked in her breath, never tiring of the view. Lake Michigan spread out in front of her, an immense sea of moody blue-gray water empowering the sand, the sky, the trees, and the birds with the energy of the goddess.

"Good morning, Lady," whispered the woman as she set her basket down on a smooth patch of sand well away from the crashing waves. She took a dark-green wool blanket from the basket and laid it out on the sand, anchoring each corner with a large beach stone. The familiar scent of lavender and mothballs wafted past her—the smell of her blanket chest picked up and carried into the pine forest by the wind to be added to the story of the place.

Sitting down with her legs spread, she pulled the basket toward her and continued to remove the contents: a small loaf of bread that she had baked the night before, a green glass bottle that held the last of the blackberry wine purchased the previous autumn from the elderly couple who lived down the road from her, a small cellar of salt, the snowy white swan feather found along the lake last summer, a sparkling blue cordial glass used in gatherings like this from a time before she was born, a homely knife whose ancient horn handle was smoothed and yellowed with age and use. Next out, a lighter, a bottle of lamp oil, and, finally, the oil lamp that would hold the place of honor in her observances here today, wrapped carefully in layers of lavender tissue.

While she was familiar with the Neo-Pagan and Wiccan altar arrangements currently used and found them to be visually inspiring and pretty, this morning's altar would reflect practices far older than the newer magical systems, its means and ways passed from grandmother, to mother, to daughter, and on down the line of women in her family. While occasionally adapted for living conditions, locations, and times, the heart of the ancient practice survived the passage of time.

She placed the blue cordial glass to her left, the cellar of salt to her right, and the swan's feather at her back, held in place with another beach stone. In front of her, she laid the loaf of bread, the wine, the lamp, and the knife. After filling the lamp with oil and setting the wick, she took the empty cordial glass to the edge of the lake and scooped up the curl of a wave just before it broke onto her legs. Laughing and jumping back quickly, the woman sketched a playful salute to the waters, knowing that next time she might not be so lucky; an icy baptism was due.

Windblown and happy, the woman settled herself back onto the scratchy wool blanket and surveyed her setup. Satisfied that it would be approved by any one of her grandmothers or aunts, she settled herself in, dropping her energy into her lower belly and deepening her breathing to bring herself to a still center place. As she concentrated on her breath, the call of the lake receded a bit and the laughing of the gulls wheeling overhead diminished. The cold wind alone anchored her to the beach, keeping her aware of her frozen fingers and numb toes.

When the tiniest warmth of the early spring sun filtered at last through the dark of the pines at her back, she opened her eyes. Maintaining the deep, rhythmic breathing that allowed her to float between realms, she picked up the salt cellar and held it aloft, saying:

> Creature of land, hail and welcome. Bless us with abundance and stability, safety and security.

Reaching behind her, she took the swan's feather and, holding it to the wind, whispered:

> Creature of air, hail and welcome. Bless us with clear thought and inspiration, bring to us poetry and song.

She replaced the feather and reached for the blue glass goblet. Holding it in front of her, she could see the undulating waves of the lake through the delicate glass. She continued:

> Creature of water, hail and welcome. Grant us safe passage between this realm and the next, between this life and the afterlife where those who came before and those who are yet to arrive meet as one.

As the wind blew her hair and the morning sun sparked within her green eyes, the woman sat still, breathing in the presence and blessings of the three realms that had gathered at her call. When the familiar sensation of being wrapped in the warmth and comfort of the Old Ones—shining and constant no matter the location of the one who called to them—settled within her, the woman closed her eyes and stood in one smooth motion, her arms held aloft, and said:

> I call to the Bright One, Brigid of fire, of forge, and of the sacred springs! Exalted One, join us as we gather for healing and laughter, creativity and joy. As we light one flame from the next, growing ever stronger as we move throughout the realms, we give you thanks and honor for your continued presence.

She opened her eyes, pleased to see that the edges of the world around her had gone soft and wispy; it was time to light the lamp.

With the wind no longer an issue within her protected space between the worlds, the lighter produced a strong flame and ignited the lamp's wick easily. Replacing the glass chimney and trimming the cotton strip to avoid too high of a flame, the woman sat down again, set the glowing lamp in front of her, and waited. The turbulent lake and the light-gray sky of the early spring morning were barely visible beyond the boundaries of her crafted cathedral and she allowed her eyes to blur gently and distort the world beyond even more.

The green-eyed woman smiled to herself as portions of the wispy edges that surrounded her began to gather themselves together and step forward, drawn to the flame like so many moths. More and more figures stepped in from the mists and sat, stood, or squatted around the circle. When the stream of women slowed, dwindled, and then stopped, she smiled in welcome, opened her arms wide in greeting, and said:

> Spring is near and the earth awakens. I am so glad that you have
> all joined me here to celebrate and honor She Who Holds the Fire.
> Brigid gathers us as her own and we joyfully answer the call. We tend
> her flame and light the way through time and space. We are all; we
> are one; we are eternal.

As she recited the ancient words taught to her so long ago, she smiled at the women who had answered the call: pretty Anna Anderson of Perthshire in Scotland, who had brought the family across the ocean; and stern Lois who, with her keen business sense, encouraged her husband's shipping business and purchased the property that became the family home in the northern reaches of America. Smiling and chatting with each other, Hannah and her great-great-grandmother, Anne, could have been poster girls for the lineage, with their bright green eyes and slight builds made even more diminutive by the bulky woolen plaids and skirts that they wore.

Back in the shadows, barely discernible from the mists that surrounded them, the small Dark Ones gathered. These women came from a time before there were nations or countries. Tiny and fierce and marked with the sacred blue of woad, draped in the skins of the stag and the doe, these women hunted and fought and forged the way for those who followed. And while they were held in high esteem and revered by the rest, their desire to stay at the edges had always been honored and had never been questioned. Some burned bright and some smoldered; it was the way of things.

The women of the family, gathered by the call of the current keeper of Brigid's flame, represented generations of love, devotion, and faith—faith in themselves and in their families, and faith in the goddess from whom they drew their collective strength.

The woman's own grandmother, Lydia, stepped forward and smiled down at her.

"Shall I pass round the wine?" she asked her granddaughter with a gentle smile.

"I would love that," she replied, holding the green glass bottle out to the tall, willowy blond.

As Lydia moved around the group, pouring wine into flasks, flagons, horns, and cups, the woman cut the loaf of dark bread with the knife first crafted by Aoife from a horn of the sacred stag brought down before the Romans came to the Isles. The woman passed the carved loaf to the fierce huntress, who passed it around to those who had gathered. None could imagine a time when Aoife had not performed this rite.

The woman stood and held the bottle of wine over her head.

"May you never thirst!" she shouted joyously and took a healthy drink of the dark liquid.

"May you never thirst!" cried the gathered women in response.

Holding a slice of the crusty bread, she cried: "May you never hunger!"

And the blessing was shouted back in Gaelic, French, English, and the unknown tongues from the darkest recesses of time and place.

Finally, the woman picked up the lamp, its flame burning brightly. The gathered generations of her blood filed past. Some smiled into the flame; some touched her on her forehead or hand; some had tears in their eyes; and some stared off into an unknown distance. But all gathered love and fellowship from the flame while sending their strength back into the dancing yellows and oranges that illuminated and strengthened their line.

When all had passed and tended to the flame, they gathered close to the petite woman with laughing green eyes bundled in wool and down. Generations of wisdom and love, strength and creativity, smiled down on the one who now held the lamp and kept the way open for them.

With her soft brown hair piled high on her head, the delicate figure of Lillian Mae stepped forward. Dressed in an Edwardian morning gown, her green eyes dancing with glee, Grandma Lil placed one small, gloved hand on the woman's belly.

"Amelia, it will be a girl."

And the love and pride of her mothers and grandmothers and sisters flowed around and through Amelia as the bright flame of Brigid shone down through the ages and forward into the future, binding and strengthening the women who tended it.

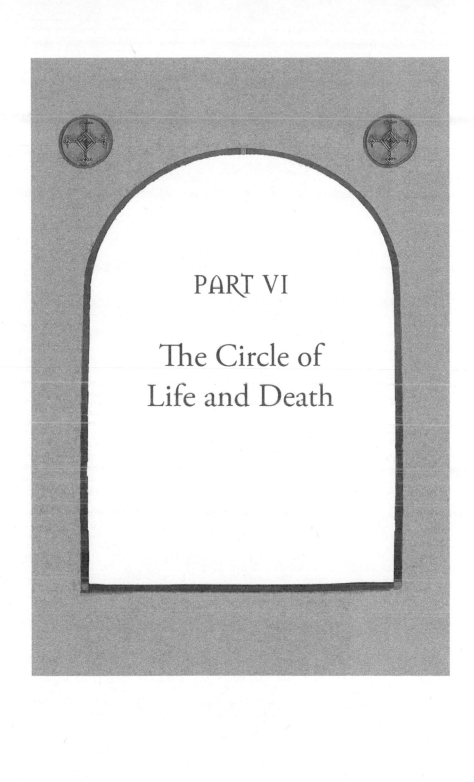

PART VI

The Circle of
Life and Death

Brigit the Midwife

Angie Buchanan

Everywhere there is life, there is song. Humans are meant to live in harmony, our unique and individual notes resounding within the symphony of life. The world needs both the bitter and the joyful melody. The songs of life and the songs of death. The essence of Brigit is both.

As a Pagan, I do not work with deity, but I do recognize the existence of "Other" and the energetic imprint those archetypal patterns and the symbols that represent them can produce in the world of human existence. I believe Brigit exemplifies this.

We mostly hear about Brigit in the early spring, at the quickening, just as the seed begins to stir in the earth. For most Pagans, she is associated with Imbolc, which begins on the eve of February 1st. Imbolc is when the "milk comes in" and the ewes are ready to begin their cycle of lambing. Brigit helps with the birthing of the lambs. She is the patron saint of mothers and childbirth and midwives. But there are many ways to give birth, and many beings do it.

Above all else, Brigit is the one who stands between, the one who inhabits the liminal spaces—the threshold that exists after the last exhale and before the next inhale. But that threshold is a busy place, and there is more than one kind of midwife.

Brigit has also been claimed as the goddess of poetry (also a form of birth), of healing, of art, and of fire and the forge. Yet fire is life, and death is the extinguishing of that fire. Brigit is thus also a death midwife, although her death midwifery is something that often gets overlooked. Because I am also a death midwife, however, it is the facet of her that intrigues me the most. On every level, where there is birth, there is death. Those of us who work in the liminal spaces of the threshold will tell you that it is the same place—that birth and death happen in the same space, and sometimes simultaneously. Beings coming in; beings going out.

The essence of liminality lies in the process of being in-between, of passing through or over a threshold, of crossing a border—the delineation that separates one place from another. It is a moment of transition from one place, or from one state of being, to another. The space of the threshold expands or contracts according to the needs of the one passing through, and the time spent there is also specific to the individual. Midwives are, by nature, shepherds through that liminal space. They are the psychopomps, the agents of transition from this life to the next. They stand present to assist both the newly born and the dying.

In her multiple manifestations—as goddess, as saint, and as bishop—Brigit suffered many losses, including the death of her son, which is something I also share. She was the protectress of cemeteries, which can be found at many of the sites that are holy to her. In addition to these associations, she is also identified as the goddess of keening, and as the originator of the art. The *Book of Invasions*, an origin legend of the Irish people that can be traced back to the seventh century, states: "Bríg came and keened for her son. At first, she shrieked, in the end she wept. Then, for the first time weeping and lamentation were heard in Ireland."

Deep grieving is a release of immediate, profound sadness. It can sometimes manifest instinctively, as a raw scream or cry. This cry is frequently the first reaction of the bereaved to news of death. Grief often manifests as the howling, the screaming, the unrestrained wailing that comes from deep within the belly of the bereaved. It is a sound that emanates from the center and evolves slowly and steadily. It is the burden of sadness, the unbearable weight of loss. But this is only the precursor of keening—the song of death.

Keening is the ritualistic practice of vocally mourning the dead. It is used as a verb—*to keen,* as in the act of lamenting—but it has also been used as a noun—*the keen,* meaning the song of death itself. Thus keening is what the Irish call the mourning ritual for the dead. It literally translates to "a lament for the dead."

Historically, keening has been a woman's tradition. Its role was to mark death as a rite of passage, and to allow the expression of grief through ritual that provided a cathartic experience. Keening enabled the unfettered purging of sorrow; it drew a line between the sacred and the mundane, the civil and the feral. Only after such a purging was someone able to move forward with life.

Today, keening is often confused with howling grief. In Ireland, however, keening had a different, deeper meaning that was based on ancient ritual. Although the original instinct of howling grief may be at its core, the keen itself was more intentional. It was a sacred improvised chant that evolved over thousands of years to consist of different sounds and cadences. It was traditionally sung over the body of the deceased by women who were trained in the art and it was fundamental to the funeral rite.

Keening held space in the liminal, at the threshold, for the initiation and the transition that constitutes the final rite of passage that is death. Moreover, this initiation and transition belonged, not only to the deceased, but also to their loved ones and their community. The bereaved are by nature in a liminal state, because they are between a former identity and a future one. They are between roles. The wife becomes the widow; the child becomes the orphan; the friend now walks the world bereft of friendship. A piece of the heart is missing; it is a painful amputation.

The women conducting the keen were the embodiments of the psychopomp—those who escort souls to the next life. It was customary for the keening to occur over the body, rising and falling, and beginning again each time a newcomer entered the space. The sound of this song served to evoke an almost involuntary release of grief from others. It held the threshold open, made it accessible; and it continued until the bereaved completed their crying.

In the 17th century, the Catholic Church moved to ban keening, viewing it as Pagan and undignified. By the early 20th century, keening was no longer used at funerals. It is a song we have forgotten. We have been robbed of the completeness of our grief in Western civilization. And as a society and a culture, we are suffering because of it.

Since 2008, my community, Earth Traditions, has held a Samhain ritual each year in which particular community members keen in order to hold the space for the grieving. It is the one time of year that we carve out to honor our beloved dead and those ancestors for whom we still nurse the wounds of loss. In a culture where crying generally denotes weakness and loss of control, this liminal space becomes a safe haven, a time of respite that my community anticipates all year.

What we have discovered at this threshold, in this liminal place, is that the pain of those experiencing recent loss transmutes into the pain of the group. The pain of the widow becomes my pain, and it is her tears that stream down my face as I raise my voice to join in the death song. It is almost involuntary, and the cacophony of voices rising and falling and blending brings forth the spirits of comfort and compassion and healing.

In that moment of pure, natural poetry, the fire of Brigit's forge is tempered by the waters of her holy wells, which are, in and of themselves, seen as portals between the worlds of form and spirit. The waters of these places designated to Brigit represent tears, birth waters, and purification. Passing through these portals, we all become new mothers, tenderly holding a newborn sense of wonder and a delicate new way of being. It is a remarkable experience.

What Brigit teaches us in her unique and inimitable way is that the wisdom and the integrity of the ancient traditions still hold fast, and still have value. Traditions may change and the world may shift into new technologies and new definitions of what is or is not appropriate behavior, but the human need to express emotional pain, to release grief, is essential and will always remain.

Now more than ever in the wake of COVID-19, we need to revisit our current grief practices. Western civilization has forgotten how to employ the lament as a cathartic tool for spiritual healing. We have forgotten how to let go and allow others to lead us into those shadowed valleys where we can purge and recover enough to begin to heal. We are a culture in crisis, in a world that is grieving. And there is a tidal wave of grief yet to come, from those who have had to suppress their grief in order to survive and to help others to survive.

The victims of illness and of violence in our troubled society need help navigating their grief and their loss—as do those who help them and tend to them. These are the real walking wounded of a war we never anticipated. Their eyes have seen more than any eyes should see. There is only so much grief the human spirit can hold before it breaks.

The wise women and the sages of the world know the importance of keeping ancient traditions alive. There is room for Brigit's voice in our world right now. From the lands of the *Tuatha Dé Danann*, she brought us keening. But because of keening's intimate nature and the superstitions attached to it, it has become increasingly difficult to find examples of this art. We can still find it referred to by small, closed communities in Ireland, although no one admits to still practicing it. There are, however, indications that keening is still practiced by some communities of Irish immigrants deep in the hills of Appalachia and examples of it can be found on the Internet (see *https://sounds.bl.uk/World-and-traditional-music*).

Perhaps we need to contemplate a revival of keening, as well as of other authentic expressions of grief, and use them as vehicles by which we can safely engage our emotions. Perhaps it is time to re-craft our current, socially accepted funerary norms and give ourselves permission to tap into the wisdom of our ancestors. These ancient traditions can provide a foundation upon which we can build healthy rituals that can help us mourn our dead and address other losses in our lives.

Our self-conscious, death-denying culture has contributed to the harboring of unexpressed pain and anguish in the human psyche. It has fostered generations of people who deny their own mortality and view the deaths of others as something distasteful and awkward, something to be avoided. Our children are largely unaware of what death means or how to navigate it. Yet the ways of Brigit are still as relevant as they ever were, and perhaps they may return just in time to save us from ourselves.

Hail Brigit!

Brighid of Keening

Jenne Micale

You didn't blame Ruadan as you bowed your head
low, the willow branches of your hair swinging,
rocking with the gale of your sobs, every
flower dropping its bloom, every egg webbed with cracks
for the ending of what should have spun forward
into time and light

Sometimes sons are swept up in waves of words
and choose the wrong side, enraptured by spears,
the graceful pass of a blade, that wonderment
when a star winks out. Every child has this
rage hatching in their core. We raise it up
into time and light

or train it like a vine to more useful ends.
The knowledge of this racks you too, how you,
the poetess, spoke the truth to him clearly
and still he laughed and picked up the spear. Even
the smith could see through the ruse as he threw it
into time and light

and how that chosen victim wouldn't consent
and instead plucked a barbed insult from the air
and flung it back. You howl, your white neck showing,
as you replay the act: a brother slaying
a son, a salt well pulling tears from the deep
into time and light

because in the end, there are no sides but this:
We who are bound by time and those beyond
it, we who yet walk in day and those who dip
over the rim and out of sight. Those we can reach
and those beyond the touch of even tears
into time and light.

Figure 18. *She Who Dwells Between the Worlds*. A self-portrait along the bank of the Garavogue River, Sligo, Ireland. Conceived as part of a visual story and as an individual window into the liminal world. Photo by Chantal Simon.

Brigid's Light

The Fire in My Medicine

Holly V. MacKenna

"She was a Catholic and a Pagan; she brought the two worlds together. Oh, and she was very beautiful. She actually prayed for God to make her more homely so all the men would leave her alone. She's perfect for you." I first learned about Brigid of Kildare from my dad when I was seventeen and needed to declare a confirmation name. At that point, I had started exploring Paganism and had fully absorbed the entire Avalon series. I was confirming my Catholicism partly because that's what an Irish Catholic does and partly because I was all about the buffet-style Catholicism my parents allowed during my teenage years.

My parents emigrated from Ireland in 1969 after getting married. They had planned to come over only for Dad to complete his obstetrics residency and to, as they say, "pay off debts." My dad ended up applying for a long-shot fellowship in maternal fetal medicine at Duke University, which he got because they reached out to an old professor at University College Dublin (UCD) who remembered my father fondly as the young man who sat and kept him company over tea breaks. My dad entered high-risk pregnancy management because he wholeheartedly believed that women did not need his help to give birth unless something was out of the ordinary. He often said women are the stronger sex and should be honored as such. I think his favorite Aunt Bridie (short for Brigid) may have had something to do with this view. She was a nurse and was, from all accounts, fierce. I still have a sweater she knitted for him that I keep in a drawer—one of the items that I claimed after he died.

I grew up following my dad around everywhere, including into the hospital. I did science projects on ultrasounds and watched as he performed high-risk procedures. When I entered medical school, I leaned on his wisdom, although I didn't understand a lot of it until much later after he was gone. My mother was and is, as Dad would say, The Boss. She was the Irish mother no kid on our block would dare talk back to, but they all adored her and now chat happily with her on the phone when called. Both of my parents encouraged me to reach for whatever goal I wanted and not look back.

I began traveling to Ireland as a babe in my mom's arms, initially to see all my twentysomething cousins and aunts and uncles. As a teen, I returned to Ireland alone and stayed with my parents' families and friends. I soon realized that Ireland held a magic that completed me. I was able to be myself there, to laugh loudly and to speak my truth. My grandfather Jack lived in the house where my father had grown up in Castledermot, County Kildare, and he was always a part of every visit. On my twenty-first birthday, when I was studying abroad for a semester at UCD, my dad rented out a farmhouse restaurant in Castledermot so Jack could waltz with his granddaughter. He also sang to me and was an immediate favorite of all my Dublin friends.

While I was at UCD, I joined the archaeological society. I did so mainly to go on a trip visiting sites over the break, but it also allowed me time to learn more about my heritage. I realized Mother Brigid and her power over the land were part of what strengthened me with each visit. Her magic lifted me up as I evolved as a woman and embraced my role as healer.

I returned to Ireland while in medical school to shadow a rural general practitioner in Kildare. He had gone to medical school with my dad and was kind enough to agree to having a young American student accompany him in clinic and on house calls over lunchtime. His kindness and gentle persona greatly influenced my view of what a physician should be. It reminded me of my father's gentleness with his high-risk patients when I was growing up and watching his every move. One visit still sticks with me even now, over twenty years later.

An older woman came in to be seen. Before we entered the examination room, however, the doctor paused and said: "Holly, do you mind terribly sitting this one out? You see, I've asked her to come in because her husband died last week. We are really just checking in and having a chat." With that, his assistant walked by with cups of tea for him and his newly widowed patient. On her way out, the assistant took my hand and said: "Come now, love, I've made us a cuppa as well." I think back now to when my father died and how my path could have been so much easier had someone made me a cuppa and offered to chat.

My father died on July 6, 2005, and my mother, brother, and I returned to Kildare a few weeks later with his ashes, which were buried in a ceremony called a "month's mind"—a requiem Mass celebrated about one month after a death in memory of the deceased. My mother and I remained there with various family members for a few weeks of respite. My dad's younger brother, John, agreed to take me to Saint Brigid's well in Kildare to retrieve some water to bring back to New Orleans, where I had a few weeks remaining in my training as a psychiatrist. I remember burying the old plastic soda bottle, which was taped shut, in my checked baggage and praying that it wouldn't leak. Little did I know that having it on my mantel would protect my apartment from the rain and floodwaters that inundated my city when Katrina hit only weeks later.

In the years following Katrina and my dad's passing, I was a bit lost. I had trained initially in pediatrics, only to realize that it wasn't the best fit for my passion for healing. Instead, I trained in psychiatry in a program that focused on therapy, which allowed me to excel. After Katrina, I also found a woman healer to help me navigate that time and my father's death.

After falling in and out of dysfunctional romantic relationships, I accepted a friend's invitation to meet at a dive bar in New Orleans' Irish Channel neighborhood. There, I met a man who turned out to be the love of my life. We were married a year later and spent much of our honeymoon in Dublin, Kildare, and Clare. I brought him to see Brigid's well in Clare, and we got more sacred water. We saw the candles that were always lit and the mementos of ancestors left by those who passed through. We tied ribbons in the trees to honor the goddess in hopes that we would be blessed. I met some elderly Irish women and told them how Brigid's water had been in my apartment when Katrina hit, and that I believed she had protected me. "Oh she did, child," they assured me. "She is always with those who travel from here."

I turned to Brigid when my husband and I lost our first pregnancy to a ruptured ectopic and I was rushed into emergency surgery. I prayed to her to help me become a mother and to keep me safe. A month after the surgery, we were pregnant with our daughter, Maeve. A few years later, we decided to try to have another child. I suffered loss after loss and thought of my grandmother, who I knew had experienced numerous losses from the stories told to me. The anguish and fear of leaving my daughter without a mother, as well as my longing for the soul I knew was meant to join me in this time and place, haunted me. Then, during my seventh pregnancy, a friend lit a candle blessed with water I gave her from Brigid's well. She placed it in a cow's pelvic bone and kept it lit until my son was born. We named him Nicholas Jarlath for our deceased fathers and call him Jack for my grandfather.

While I struggled to become pregnant with my son, I began leaning into non-Western ways of healing. I engaged in meditation, which I had first learned in Ireland as a student. I found an acupuncturist and started paying closer attention to my body and spirit. After Jack was born, I began actively pursuing more training in integrative medicine. At that point, I was in a leadership position I had struggled to obtain and was comfortable financially.

It was then I realized that the traditional role of a doctor no longer suited me. I was no longer satisfied with simply prescribing a pill and moving on to the next patient. I found myself thinking back to my times in Kildare with the country GP performing house calls and truly meeting people where they were in their lives and their health. I started feeling like an outsider, uncomfortable and unwelcome among my peers and supervisors. I couldn't stop feeling that I wanted to offer healing in a different way. Brigid's fire had been lit and there was no squelching it.

I decided I had to make a choice. I could stay as I was—financially comfortable, but spiritually dying, pushing pills and closing off my inner fire—or I could let it all burn and start again from the embers. I did my best to resist my calling, but the universe and my spiritual guides wouldn't stop pushing until I gave in.

When I decided to leave my traditional medical practice, I reached out to my family in Ireland—to my father's brother and a cousin from my mother's side. I asked them both for ideas about what to name my practice. I mentioned my desire to honor the oak trees that stood strong in New Orleans during Katrina and back home in Ireland where my ancestors slept. Both referenced the roots of Kildare's name in Irish: *Cill Dara*, or "church of the oak"—named for Brigid and her original sanctuary. I took the name for my new healing sanctuary: Dara Wellness.

I opened Dara Wellness in March 2020. The first COVID-19 case hit New Orleans a week later. As businesses began to shut down and people started isolating, I panicked. I wondered if I had been too rash in my choice to enter private practice and risk everything. Then I stepped back and took a deep look at my values. I asked myself what it was that had driven me to become a healer in the first place.

I remembered back to the days following Katrina when the city was regrouping. That is when I listened to my heart. I started offering free stress-management sessions to first responders. When my intention became known to others, more people began to reach out for help.

I spent the months of quarantine studying integrative medicine and connecting with other healers. I met mediums and spiritual guides, Native American medicine men, and meditation teachers. I entered guided journeys in which I embraced my ancestors—some of whom I recognized, but many of whom I did not.

One such encounter was led by a trusted teacher. I was advised to go to my ancestors for guidance. I found myself in the Burren, an area of northwestern County Clare dominated by a moonlike landscape of gray rock etched with crevices and cracks. I stood in a fairy circle made long ago by the wise folk, surrounded by vast stretches of limestone. As the sun set, the spirits of my ancestral guides appeared around me and a woman stepped forth. I saw her long red braid and blue *Cill Dara* tartan and knew she was Brigid. She encouraged me to continue on my own path, using my talents as a healer in new ways. She and the others made it clear that they would always be with me.

A few months later, I was blessed to take part in a shamanic journey and again entered the realm beyond the veil. Brigid led me through the darkness to a fire. It burned warmly on my face as the embers sparked at my feet. Again, I knew I was surrounded by love and support on my path.

In the months that followed, I embraced my feminine energy and stopped trying to "do" in favor of being present for myself and those who sought me out for care. I began to feel the spiritual energy in my daily existence and connection came more easily.

I continue now on my journey as a healer, a mother, a woman. As I tuck my daughter into bed each night, I give her a favorite stuffed animal. On it is a piece of green and white yarn—yarn we placed outside our home on a bush on the eve of February 1st, to be blessed by Brigid that night as she passed our home.

The Guiding Star

NíDara

The beauteous brooch,
the brilliant star that adorns Your emerald mantle,
guides me through the past, present, and future.

Tangled threads of the family tapestry,
forgotten traditions and lore,
do not dull the radiance of Your shining beacon.

Old texts and bits of archaeology
ignite my adoration of who You are,
Lady of Poetry, Smithcraft, and Medicine.

Saint and Goddess,
Walker between Lands and Realms,
You bring peoples together.

Primal Fire and Primordial Waters
bind together as one,
entwining to inspire, heal, and create.

Old traditions blend with the new,
weaving together a vibrant fabric,
a unique cloak of liminality.

The star's light from the past
illuminates my path to the present,
forging my relationship with You.

Your stories of then and now,
the mythical tales of there and here,
show me how to honor You.

Your divine inspiration
stirs my hands
to weave, paint, draw, and write.

Your compassion
warms my heart to action,
to help where I can.

Your sacred flame
kindles my soul
as I tend the flame.

I feel You reshaping me,
an ingot upon Your anvil,
malleable and full of potential.

What will You craft me into?
What shape will I have?
Am I strong enough to endure the process?

My faith in You is a lantern,
lighting my course through the darkness,
a luminous companion.

The candle flickers,
sometimes steady,
occasionally wavering.

The journey becomes one of contemplation,
of mysticism and deep study,
onward into a great spiral.

The further I go,
the more I know You,
understanding Your epiphanic Mysteries.

The blazing ember in the sky,
the shining jewel pinned to Your cloak,
brightens my path to the future.

Maman Brijit

Raven Morgaine

Brighid, Celtic goddess and Christian saint, was brought to new lands by white Irish, Scottish, and English women who had been sentenced to indentured servitude. Having broken some law or committed some crime, these women were often poor and alone, and had no one to pay their fines. So they were packed off to "masters" abroad to work off their debt—something which, in actuality, they could never really do. These women carried their protector, Brighid, with them to Haiti, where she met her African counterpart, Maman Brijit. Both these spirits were associated with justice and fire. Maman, however, was a *lwa* (spirit) of death and Queen of the Dead. Enslaved Africans syncretized her with Saint Brighid, whose pale skin and red hair became her Catholic mask.

Maman Brijit rules over the cemetery and the dead, and can usually be found by any tomb marked with a cross, although she always haunts the grave of the first woman buried in any graveyard, joined by her husband, Baron Samedi, a *lwa* of death, sex, and resurrection. The two share a penchant for vulgarity and lewdness. Maman Brijit is considered equal in power to her consort and they are the only *lwa* who do not depend on ceremonies to cross into the world of living humans.

Like Baron Samedi, Maman Brijit can turn the tide of terminal illnesses if she chooses to. When she doesn't, she leads the soul of the departed to the next world. I created this painting (Figure 19) a few years ago as an offering and tribute to Maman for retrieving a good friend from the brink of death.

Brijit is typically portrayed with white skin and red hair, but I do not usually paint her that way, as Brighid the goddess and Brijit the *lwa* are two distinct spirits. I chose to paint her as dark-skinned with ebony hair to reflect her African roots. I do, however, portray her with the ceremonial chalky white-powdered face traditionally associated with the dead. This painting shows her with two sets of irises in her eyes to represent her ability to see into all realms at once.

Figure 19. *Maman Brijit,* portrayed as the *lwa* (spirit) of death and Queen of the Dead. She rules over the cemetery and the dead, and can usually be found by any tomb marked with a cross, although she always haunts the grave of the first woman buried in any graveyard, joined by her husband, Baron Samedi, a *lwa* of death, sex, and resurrection. Painting by Raven Morgaine.

Look with the Wolf's Eyes

Donna Gerrard

Spirit of White Wolf be mine.
Walk toward me, sweet canine of white.
Shapeshift into me and let us unite.
Through me, let White Wolf spirit shine.

Vision of White Wolf be mine.
Together let our vision see
All that is living and dead and yet to be.
Through me, let White Wolf vision shine.

Invisibility of White Wolf be mine.
Bring Crone Brighid's winter snow
To cover our tracks wherever we go.
Through me, let White Wolf invisibility shine.

Magic of White Wolf be mine.
Together beyond the veil we can move
And circle with the ancestors in protection and love.
Through me let White Wolf magic shine.

Spirit of White Wolf be mine.
We walk together in authenticity.
We are the Wolf. We look with White Wolf's eyes.
Through me, let White Wolf spirit shine.

My Personal Relationship with Brid

Bernadette Montana

My relationship with Brid has always been a personal one, although not always an easy or, shall we say, a happy one.

When I think of Brid, my mind immediately goes to a mother figure. That does not always mean being sweet or endearing, however. Sometimes it means being tough and strong. More times than not, that is who she is for me. A deity who has kicked my butt on more than a few occasions, in order to get a message through to me. It's almost clichéd to say that she picked me, or that I picked her. I am really not so sure who picked whom! Drawn to her energy is a better description. I attribute to her my love for the arts, music, science, psychology, and the fiber arts. Brid guides me.

I was blessed to be able to visit Brid's shrine in Ireland on three occasions with my husband, Thomas, and one of my initiates, Chandra. We were also blessed with the ability to stay with my high priestess and high priest, Janet Farrar and Gavin Bone. With them to act as tour guides, we were able to experience Brid's ancestral land. Going to her well, making devotions to her, and cleansing myself in her waters brought me to tears. Never will I forget her blessing me that day. It was as if she were preparing me for something.

Life has never been easy for me. My mother is of Sicilian/Irish heritage, my father of Puerto Rican/Taino ancestry. There was something to be said about being raised in such a diverse cultural mix. We were raised to understand that dying is a part of life. It was always talked about. My three younger sisters and I understood this. Maybe it's a generational thing.

Lady Brid has always been there for me—so much so that, when I decided to open my own metaphysical store, I named it Brid's Closet. I do tarot readings, teach classes, and counsel people through the many kinds of spiritual crises they experience in their lives. Many of these sessions involve the passing of family members and loved ones. Some of the ways in which I help these amazing people is through mediumship or by simply listening to them. Much of the advice I give comes from my own experiences, or from information I have learned over all these many years.

I have three amazing sons. They are all talented and smart. But I dedicate these words to one in particular—my son Alexander Montana Lefkowitz. It is because of him that I developed an even stronger relationship with Brid.

Alex was very intelligent, with a wicked sense of humor. On the high end of the ADHD spectrum, he had a tough time with people in general and spoke with a stutter. Yet he was able to land some amazing jobs as a computer programmer, writing code for applications and games. In order to cope with his ADHD, he began using drugs, introduced to him by a former colleague.

We had not heard from him in two days. We checked his phone records—no calls. We found him in his room. Accidental overdose was the official verdict—acute fentanyl poisoning. This was the worst day of my life. Not only did he die alone; I had not been there to bless him. My husband caught me as I fainted. The police told me to sit in my husband's truck to spare me the trauma of identifying my son. The song that came on the radio made me cry even more. It was a song I used to sing to my sons as babies.

Alex was not a believer, but it was his death that brought me closer to Brid than I had ever been. I was furious with her, yet sought her help at the same time. I yelled at her, screamed my heart out at her, both at home and at my store. Never had I been in so much pain.

But there was no time for grief. I had to get all the legalities taken care of. I had to plan Alex's cremation and memorial service. I had to be there for my other two sons, Jonathan and Andrew, as well as to comfort their father (who is family to me). And somehow I had to support my husband, who literally had to pick up the pieces of what was left of me.

I was angry. Mad. Livid. Broken.

When all this craziness calmed down, the need to talk with Brid was strong within me. So I locked the door to my store, brought out my tarot deck, lit a candle, burned some incense, and just waited. I shuffled the deck and drew a couple of cards, just hoping to see if I could get a message. It was then that I heard her.

She said that she had been with my son when he was born (Mother's Day weekend), and with him when he died (Father's Day/Litha weekend). She told me that this was all a process I had to go through, and that my crying and keening were a part of that process—both as a dedicant of hers and as a mother. She said that I had helped many others with the passing of loved ones, but that now I needed to understand that pain.

I screamed (again), yelled, threw books around the store, and lay on the floor crying for what seemed like an eternity. What do I do now? How do I accept this? What do I do with this information?

It's been three years now. I ask Brid to hold him tight; I ask that he may now be happy. And I use his story to help others in service to my Lady. Talking to people about death is never easy, but they now know that I have been through this pain and survived it as well. I stand as an example that faith has a way of pissing you off, but making you a better person.

I still talk to Alex often. And, in my prayers, I still quietly sing him the song that I heard that night—"Do You Want to Know a Secret?" by the Beatles.

Lady Brid sets the bar for me. Her stories of strength resonate with me. Now that I am a crone, I share the wisdom I have gained. To know that she was there for my son comforts me. She is a source of energy for me. My daily practice is far less formal than it used to be. Somehow it feels more "real" now. When I garden, I talk to Brid. When I sing, I sing to Brid. When I craft, I ask her for inspiration and blessings. I leave the roses that I grow on her altar. Her roles as midwife, healer, crafter, artist, and smith are all inspirational to me. She has taught me to embrace my grief, just as when she cried and keened at the loss of her own son, Ruadan. She knows my anguish, and I now understand hers.

Very personal indeed.

Offering of Tears

Rowan Taw

I can think of no higher offering than an offering of tears.
Not cold, bitter tears of pain and anguish,
for Brigid has removed the need for keening.
The tears of the offering are warm,
forged in Brigid's flame of emotional support.
The tears of the offering are salty
from the ocean of healing provided by Brigid's waters.
The tears of the offering are Brigid's poetry—
enacted in a natural expression of love.
I offer these tears to Brigid, Brigid the blacksmith,
I offer these tears to Brigid, Brigid the healer,
I offer these tears to Brigid, Brigid the poet.
I offer myself to Brigid, for she is all things and never apart from me.

Laying Brigid's Bones

Kimberly Moore

My maternal great-grandmother, Rose O'Neal, was raised in a Catholic orphanage in Ireland and immigrated to New York, where she met my great-grandfather, who had come to America from Germany as a child. Her early life has remained something of a mystery because the church and all its records were destroyed in a fire and she rarely shared any information about her childhood.

Rose brought twelve children into this world; my grandmother was the eldest of the ten that survived. My great-grandfather was a domineering man with a drinking problem who died when I was a baby. By all family accounts, Rose did not have an easy life, but her children always rallied around her. She lived next door to her oldest son and just a short walk from four of her children. The rest lived within a ten-minute drive.

What I remember about my great-grandmother is that she smelled like lavender and bread, and had a great bosom for kid cuddles. Rose had a gentle spirit and was soft-spoken, with a distinct Irish brogue. Something was always cooking in her kitchen and, when I visited her, she made me tea and listened to me chatter practically nonstop. I was nine years old when she died. I'll never forget the day.

As I stood in a long, dark hospital hallway beside her hospital bed, I saw my great-grandmother rise and walk away. As she did so, she looked at me once over her shoulder and smiled. Then she walked down the hallway until she disappeared. Everyone told me it was just a dream.

Rose's wake was the first I had ever attended. I sat with a favorite uncle who didn't mind my intense curiosity and questions about the event. As Rose's eldest child, my grandmother sat front and center at the casket, the embodiment of the matriarch. Hundreds of people came that evening and each one stopped to speak to her. My grandmother was unflappable, even when one of her younger sisters wailed and threw herself at the casket. She crisply ordered some cousins to carry my aunt to another room to compose herself and continued greeting the long line of mourners.

Some relatives stopped where I was seated to ask me about my dream. Word travels fast in big families. I repeated what I had seen and then watched as they looked over my head at my uncle as if I had said something significant. When I asked my uncle why, he explained that my great-grandmother had sometimes had dreams or premonitions of things that were about to happen. I tucked that knowledge into my heart and, perhaps, that was the day that I started laying Brigid's bones.

My mother worked evenings and nights as a nurse, so I spent a lot of time with my grandmother. Even now, I can close my eyes and see myself in her kitchen. I hear the busy clanging of pots. I smell the enticing, rich aromas of chicken and fresh vegetables in the pot being prepped for a dinner of chicken and dumplings. I revel in the undertones of molasses melting in the oven. One pie sits on the windowsill to cool and I hear the oven door open to receive the next one, intended for a sick neighbor. Her absentminded murmurs embrace me, her litanies of to-dos while she peels potatoes: "We have to go to Zook's to pick up tomatoes and beans, then stop by Stoltzfus' for meat, and take the pie to Mrs. Cole I made cookies for the firehouse, so don't let me forget them."

I nod in the vision to stay in this embrace, in this moment in my grandmother's kitchen. My hand brushes the plastic tablecloth and sweeps away some stray crumbs from her coffee and toast. The radio buzzes in the background and a horn beeps as a cousin drives by the house. I know the spots where the linoleum floor dips slightly. I know the feel of her coffee cups. And I know that, if I walk up behind her and put my arms around her, she will stop and cross her arms for a moment over mine before bustling off to get things ready to deliver. Outside, the laundry flaps in a light breeze, the sun dapples through the immense oak tree, and all of these things coalesce in my heart as home.

Not a birth, illness, or death happened in our family or in the local community for which my grandmother did not make a blanket or food, or stop by to help. She ran the Women's Auxiliary for our local firehouse for almost fifty years and was a powerful force in the world, the epitome of a matriarch. I talked to her every day of my life, even when I moved from Delaware to Florida in my early twenties.

It was in Florida that I connected with my first spiritual teacher and goddess community. Not really knowing how goddess things worked, I presumed that, with Irish and English DNA and ancestry on both sides of the family, I was wired for the Celtic goddesses. It did not happen quite like that. Hekate, the orishas, Isis, and Shakti all stepped forward vibrantly, easily. The Celts? Always available to me on behalf of someone else, but not so much for my own path.

Five years after I moved to Florida, my grandmother was diagnosed with renal failure. By then, I had my own son, who was not quite two. I dropped everything and went with the baby to stay with her for several weeks. A few days after we left her, my grandmother had a massive stroke. My mom flew up within hours and I was preparing to go the next day. That night, I had a dream that my grandmother was walking across a big field with a person on each side of her, listening to what they were saying. Then she turned her head, looked over her shoulder at me, and smiled. I sat straight up in bed, knowing she was gone. I woke the baby with my movement and he also sat up. Sleepily, he said: "Bye-bye, Nanny." Then he climbed into my lap. Five minutes later, my mom called to say she was gone.

As large as the wake and funeral for my great-grandmother had been, my grandmother's wake was triple its size. I knelt at her grave and gathered some dirt to take home with me. The remains of that dirt still sit on my ancestor altar.

Twenty-three years after I left Delaware, I felt an insistent urge to return "home." I had not been back since we had buried my grandmother sixteen years before. My cousins still live in my great-grandmother's house. More family lives in the back orchard and one of Rose's children, my great-uncle, is still alive. When I returned, I moved into a community that was down the street from where I was born. My grandmother and three of her sisters had lived there, and my parents and several uncles and cousins still did. In fact, most of my gigantic extended family still lives within a fifteen-minute drive.

Two weeks after moving into this house, I had a wild dream. I was "awake" in my dream and sat up in bed. My room was filled with goddesses. Some I recognized and some I did not, but they were all from the

Celtic lands. Brigid stood in the back with a steady smile. Another sat on my bed telling me stories about the bones in the sack she carried.

The next night, I "awoke" again and, this time, I heard people in my kitchen. It was Rose, my grandmother, and my great-aunts. I could hear them making coffee and tea. I smelled peach pie! Their conversation and laughter seemed so normal; I allowed it to ebb and flow all around me. I didn't want it to end. I shared the experiences with my godmother, who reminded me that the dreams had occurred on my great-grandmother's birthday, July 16th.

The goddess Brigid came home to me that Samhain. A student gifted me with an amazing Brigid doll handcrafted by a Scottish priestess. I sat her on my desk and stroked the wool. She began weaving her way more firmly into my heart and into MotherHouse, an online devotional community. I began placing a Brigid candle on the MotherHouse altar, anointed with her oil. When I was ill, I moved her to be near my bed. Her red hair reminded me of my grandmother and her sisters.

And then I had another dream.

I am kneeling in my grandmother's front yard, digging a small hole almost frantically. "These are my ancestral lands," I say to someone unknown standing next to me. I run into my grandmother's kitchen and grab a bowl for the cool, moist dirt. When I wake up, I keep hearing the words "ancestral lands."

Brigid now has her own altar in the kitchen of my home and a presence on several other altars. She hangs over my bed. My advanced priestess training class numbers at least five priestesses of Brigid. I often dream of my grandmother's kitchen and I can always sense Brigid when I wake from these dreams—subtle, soothing.

Two weeks before the most recent Winter Solstice, Brigid came to me again in a dream/vision. She had a bow on her back and a sickle at her waist. She was holding a sword. "Take the sword," she insisted. And who says "no" to a goddess? I took the sword from her and felt an intense influx of energy. My father died suddenly a week later and, as I sat on his porch the night he passed, I felt Brigid standing behind me with her hand on my shoulder.

In processing the grief of my father's passing, I have been sharing stories with my son, my nephews, and my niece. We laugh, we cry, we lament, and we wonder at the cycle of time and synchronicities. They now seek me out for evenings of stories and memory-sharing. And with each memory, each story, we lay Brigid's bones.

I come from a line of women who carry Brigid's bones. My bones are Brigid's bones. My child's bones are Brigid's bones. My nephews' bones are Brigid's bones. My niece's bones are Brigid's bones. Remembering where we come from, we bring that knowledge, Brigid's bones, with us into each new day to lay them again and again.

Hill of Poetry

Michael Routery

She spells me a seabird,
like a fledgling driven
from nest I fell
tossed from that bluff
into blustery winds

flying out
on gull wings
hard to do. At times
I'm barely above the waves;
such muscles birds have,
coordination, effort—
sure, there is an art
of riding winds
but that takes much time.

The ocean dark
charcoaled it is,
petrels storm about me
darting.
Lifting up again
the shore behind me
I skitter near the break of foam
and something snaps,
fearsome jaws
almost got me.
I labor upward—
I will not be taken
by that monster

and finally with the wind at my back
I hurl back to the rocks,
to the shelter of the Old Lady who lives there
and drop my wings and feathers.

Over the waves a line of pelicans, a horizon shifting.

The Healing Well

Amy Blackthorn

Brigid has a well. Not just any well, but a beautiful, blue ceramic well. I know because, you see, I died eighteen years ago. You wouldn't know it to look at me; I did eventually get over it. But I'm getting ahead of myself; let's back up.

I found witchcraft on a warm summer night when I was eleven years old. The goddess had been calling to me for years, from the pages of the encyclopedias at the school library and on the warm breeze of a summer night. That night, so many years ago, my older sister, with whom I shared a room, brought home a book along with her best friend, Christine. She admonished me to make myself scarce. And, as anyone with a younger sibling can tell you, the easiest way to get a younger sister involved in what you are doing is to tell her she isn't invited.

That night, under the cover of darkness, I crept across the room to my sister's book bag and, by the light of the moon, unzipped it to find *Wicca: A Guide for the Solitary Practitioner* by Scott Cunningham. I read it under the covers by the light from the gas station up the block. I didn't sleep a wink that night. And from then on, I made it my mission to read everything I could get my hands on about witchcraft. And that's where I found the goddess.

After reading for four years and deciding that this was the path for me, I decided to tell my family. As I planned my self-dedication, I read (agonized over) horror stories of other teens like myself who confessed their religious leanings to conservative parents and were grounded, kicked out of the house, exorcized, or worse. My strategy involved first coming out of the broom closet to my mother's maternal cousin, whom we called Peep. I steeled myself and sat Peep down for a "grown-up talk." Peep had always been the person to whom I knew I could tell anything. I knew she'd always support me and be there if I needed anything. She was raised Irish Catholic, but believed that spirituality lived in your heart, not in a building.

My mother is the child of two Scots who were among those transported to Ireland and who eventually immigrated to eastern Kentucky and northeast Tennessee. Peep was very proud of her Irish roots, so much so that her home was decorated in her favorite color, green. She visited Ireland every year and brought me back treasures from the vendors along the Cliffs of Moher in County Clare where her family originated. She took the news of my religious conversion in stride and supported me as she always did, with open arms and an open heart. She asked what it meant to me to be a witch, and we bonded over our love of the goddess. Peep took me upstairs to the formal living room (only used at Christmas and New Year) and picked up my favorite photo of her and her husband, Bill—taken at Halloween, with Bill dressed as a priest and Peep dressed as a nun.

"You know, when I was younger," she said, "I saw myself as a kind of nun, in service to Saint Brigid." She was the only girl in a family of Irish and Italian immigrants, so when her parents fell ill, it was her familial obligation to care for them herself, to learn how to give them the injections that would keep them alive, and to see to their needs even before her own. She shared her love and admiration for the spirit of Brigid, whether goddess or saint, with me. It was as if we had our own secret worship of her. Coming as I did from a large family, it was liberating to feel that I had something that was just mine—something I hadn't inherited from an older sister or had to share with the younger ones.

Fast-forward three years. I was now nurturing a steadily increasing love of the divine, especially the Divine Feminine, and I decided I was ready to make it official by joining a coven. I was the youngest member, of course; most covens avoid legal entanglements by not accepting anyone underage. When I learned that the coven was part of a larger group of 500 witches who worshipped both the Morrigan and Brigid, I was over the moon. I knew this coven could help me develop the work I wanted to do for her. I was dedicated at Ostara that year, and I'd never been happier, or felt more seen.

Three years later, in October, my life changed forever. On a Thursday night, I left a date with my partner of three years and headed home. I never made it. I stopped for gas at a local gas station and grabbed a gallon of milk and a diet Pepsi for my roommate. Long story short, the next thing I knew, I was being wheeled down the hallway in a hospital emergency room. I can still see the lights passing overhead as I tried to figure out where I was and what was happening. I woke up on Saturday morning to find my roommate, my partner, my high priestess, and various other people surrounding my bed. I had two broken arms, two broken legs, a broken nose, and twenty-seven other broken bones. A network of seventy-two pins, 200 staples, and over 600 stitches was holding me together. And I was told I'd never walk again.

In the span of a few days, my full-time job went from being a florist to "getting better." Members of my coven volunteered time to come see me, to check on my progress, to offer Reiki sessions, and to bring me things I might need. On one such day, a coven mate delivered a gift from the entire group: a blue ceramic pot and a green velvet pouch. The ceramic pot contained a "lucky bamboo" plant (*Dracaena sanderiana*) and some tumbled stones. Each member of the coven had chosen two tumbled stones, charged them with a wish for my well-being, and placed one in the pot and one in the green velvet pouch. I wore the pouch under my hospital gown, and the ceramic pot became a healing well dedicated to Brigid.

Water is sacred to all life on this planet, the goddess tells us. And her message is clear: Water the well, as yourself. This blue ceramic pot thus connected me by oath, by love, and by magic to the sacred healing powers of the goddess.

When my coven was allowed to come into my (by then) private room for Samhain ritual, although my facial muscles were traumatically damaged, my inner smile reached from ear to ear. My doctors called my healing miraculous. Was I suddenly jumping out of the hospital bed, as Grandpa did in *Willy Wonka & the Chocolate Factory*? No, but it was miraculous nonetheless. For instance, a bone infection that led doctors to consider amputating my left leg was healed, so I got to keep the leg. The fight in this witch helped me ace my physical therapy despite the pain and fear.

One day, when my doctor came to my hospital room for his daily rounds, he took off his glasses, looked at me, and asked: "Do you have something to tell me? What's your secret?"

"That's easy, Doc," I replied. "Five hundred witches are praying to Brigid for me, around the clock. They're asking her to intercede on my behalf, to heal me."

"Well, it probably doesn't hurt that you were a black belt when this happened," he replied. "That gave your body something to work with. But if she's helping, I give thanks."

I still give thanks, every Monday when I pour charged water into her blue ceramic well.

Brigid's Place

Lucía Moreno-Velo

There is a well
at the edge of a field.
It sits in silence,
all but forgotten,
honored only
by a few frogs
and an archaeologist,
who visited once,
sat next to it
and ate a sandwich.

There was an altar there once,
and the bustle of a festival;
flowers were brought
and songs sung,
and food was shared.
Pebbles were dropped
in the still water
and the entrance
was kept clear
of bracken and mud.

If you walk past it,
you will probably miss it,
mistake it for a mass of rocks
at the foot of a rowan.

But shepherds know
when a lamb goes astray
to look for her there,
and small flowers
gather around it,
singing spring into life.

And the next time
the archaeologist visits,
maybe, just maybe,
she will find there,
among the early crocus,
a round cake, a straw cross,
a posy, and a prayer.

Brigid Is My Ancestor

Cairelle Crow

In early 2014, my mother gifted me and my sister, Kelly, with a small early inheritance, stipulating that we use the money for travel. "Seeing the world gives you experiences and memories no one can ever take from you," she explained. As a genealogist and my family's historian, I am a tree traveler at heart and, given a choice, will always gravitate toward visiting ancestral places. Kelly and I decided we wanted to travel together and set our sights on the summer of 2015 so we could attend a family reunion in Wales. Then we immediately entered into sisterly negotiations about where else to visit.

I was very familiar with our maternal heritage and wanted to focus our trip on France, with a side foray over to Wales for the gathering. My sister was insistent that we also put Ireland on the itinerary. She'd always felt a pull to go there, and she also wanted to drink "real Guinness." At the time of our mother's gift, we had only murky connections to Ireland in the form of vague Scots-Irish ancestors on her side. But, as a longtime devotee of Brigid, I certainly was not averse to adding a visit to Ireland to our travel plan. It had been a long-held dream of mine to walk her sacred sites.

Over the next couple of months, Kelly researched places to go and I poured myself into digging more deeply into our family tree. Other than the names of grandparents and great-grandparents, I had very little detailed knowledge of my father's roots. He and my mother had divorced when my sister and I were little girls, and we grew up without his presence in our lives, disconnected from that side of our family. Social media brought him back to me in 2008, albeit in a superficial way, but it was just enough for me to realize how much I'd lost by not having a loving father fully present in my life. Our relationship was strained, but we found common ground in genealogy. He shared with me what he knew of his family tree: Spanish and Jewish on his father's side, Welsh and Cornish on his mother's side. I was thrilled with this new information.

In 2014, as a fledgling genetic genealogist, I'd used DNA testing to help my adopted husband find his birth mother and decided to test my own DNA and that of my parents "just for fun." My mother was excited to join me on my adventure, but my father at first refused. After some cajoling by my mother, however, he finally relented. We'd just begun to explore his test results when I noticed some irregularities, namely a lack of important matches that led me to suspect he might be a "non-paternity event," commonly known among genealogists as an NPE. In simple terms, the person he knew as his dad might not be his biological father.

As I puzzled over if and how I should bring up my suspicions about his paternity, he was suddenly hospitalized in critical condition after his breathing stopped during a diagnostic procedure. A few days later, he remained on a ventilator and we were told he had an aggressive form of lung cancer. I'd helped him years earlier with an advance directive, so I was familiar with his wishes and I spent the next couple of days helping to coordinate end-of-life care with much younger siblings I didn't really know. When his time came, seventy years and four months to the day after he was born, I said goodbye to my father over the phone. It felt cold and inadequate. But I was told that his eyes flew open and his head turned when he heard my voice. The ICU nurse in me is suspicious, although the thought of it simultaneously brings me a measure of joy and pains my heart. I do know that I will never forget the ripping sensation of loss in my gut and the howl of anguish that spontaneously erupted from me when I was told he was gone.

On the rare occasions when I'd considered it, I always believed my father's death wouldn't affect me very much, mostly because he'd been so absent from my life. The reality was different, however, and it was brutal. The man responsible for half of my existence was gone in a way that could never be remedied. I was crushed, and I grieved deeply for many weeks. Brigid was at the forefront in those early days, her presence quiet, unassuming, steadfast. Every day, I wrapped up in my shawl that had been blessed by her the previous Imbolc, and I sank deep into the soft comfort of her healing love.

The prolonged intensity of my grief, coupled with the arrival of full-blown perimenopause, manifested in distressing physical symptoms that caused me to become dangerously anemic. My doctor prescribed an iron supplement and I slowly began the process of crawling out from underneath my weighty sorrow. I sat with Brigid every day, sharing with her my pain and my frustration at feeling so unwell, and thanking her for the spiritual comfort she provided. I felt nudged toward my genealogy work again and I poured my energy into planning my trip, now knowing that I'd be visiting the homelands of my father's ancestors. My sister and I settled on Cornwall and Wales, with a side trip to Ireland to accommodate my sister's quest for "real Guinness" and my own desire to visit Brigid and her sacred sites. Despite feeling exhausted and short of breath due to the anemia, I was very excited.

Just prior to our trip, I confirmed that the man my father had believed was his dad was actually not his biological father. It was anticlimactic; there was really no one to tell other than my siblings. They were interested in knowing more, and I needed answers for myself. So I made further requests for testing on the DNA sample that remained in storage and I started testing my siblings and other relatives so I could get a more complete picture of the relationships. Thus began the hard work of trying to solve the mystery of my missing grandfather.

In addition to the mundane aspects of genealogy work, I also use a multitude of magical elements when I do research. I gathered those tools and set up an altar specifically to open the way for me to discover the ancestors who were hidden behind that wall of secrecy. I could feel them there, pressing against my lack of knowledge, and their requests to "come through" stayed heavy on my mind. These were ancestors who had been waiting for me to find them. Just before I left for my trip, I lit a candle and promised I would somehow open a door to true knowledge of them. I involved Brigid in this request and asked for guidance and to be led to the truth.

Kelly and I traveled by train from our homes in New Orleans to New York City, where we spent a few days exploring the Big Apple before boarding the *Queen Mary II* for a seven-day transatlantic crossing. It was super-extravagant and had been on my bucket list for many years. We arrived in Southampton feeling refreshed by our time spent crossing the ocean. After grabbing our rental car and then dealing with the harrowing experience of me learning to drive "in English" on the roads between Southampton and Exeter, we spent a lovely few days exploring that area of Devon before heading down into Cornwall. The feeling of stepping for the first time onto Cornish soil will always stay with me. We arrived at our lodging—a gorgeous and fragrant farm complete with crops, wildflowers, stone walls, cows, and sheep—and I took off my shoes before I got out of the car. As my toes dug into the earth, tears started rolling down my face. My heart felt as if it would burst. I had no idea what was happening. I could only surmise I'd arrived in a place that felt right somehow and that my body recognized its innate belonging.

Our days in Cornwall were busy and beautiful. We went to the church attended by our Lathlean ancestors. We found their house, recently renovated, where a coin had been pressed into an old sill, presumed to have been placed there by the original builder. I braved driving miles and miles on single-track roads to cemeteries to visit ancestral graves. (Yes, I consider it bravery for my city-self to manage a single-track Cornish road filled with oncoming harvest-season tractors!) I spent hours at the Cornish Family History Society in Truro, where delightful staff helped me find answers to my questions about my Nankivell and Bonython ancestors. We explored gardens and old churches; we chanted in stone circles; we stargazed from grassy moors and cliff edges. I slowly began to realize that the particular something I couldn't quite identify that was missing from me in America was infusing itself into my being in Cornwall. Immersing myself in the culture and physically being on the land somehow reactivated a connection that was so much stronger than what I had felt when I put ancestral names and places to paper during my genealogy research.

We had a similar experience in Wales. We met up with Welsh family in Pembrokeshire and enjoyed twelve days of a nonstop guided tour hosted by a Dorset-born cousin who had an in-depth knowledge of our family history. I learned more than I ever dreamed I could know about my Picton and Rees ancestors. Brigid was with me in this rugged landscape; she is present in innumerable holy places and spaces there, and I was eagerly anticipating how I would feel in Ireland as I walked upon the land.

Sadly, however, our traveling-sisters adventure came to a sudden end. While walking down a steep road at our bed-and-breakfast in Fishguard, Wales, Kelly tripped and fell. She limped, literally, to Ireland via ferry and, a day later, was diagnosed with a broken foot. She was devastated that she needed to go home. I was sad for her, but also sad to lose my traveling companion. I took her to a local pub and bought her that "real Guinness" she craved, then bundled her off to Dublin to catch a flight home to New Orleans. Suddenly I was alone in Ireland.

The beauty of Ireland cannot be overstated in any way. It is the most luscious green land I've ever seen in my life. Every shade of green is found there; it's nearly overwhelming. I basked in its sun, its frequent and random rain showers, the smell of the air, the architecture, the history, the arcane mist that blankets the land and leaves you feeling as if you are a time-traveler. I drank beer; I drank whiskey. I ate cabbage and bacon, and indulged in rose-petal-covered chocolates. I visited wells, castles, dolmens, gardens, glens, and groves. I enjoyed live traditional music in small village pubs, rambled around the Film Fleadh in Galway, and nearly froze to death in the middle of July at the Cliffs of Moher. I did *not* kiss any stones. One memory sits deep within my soul, however—a day trip around the Ring of Kerry, a 111-mile-long circular route in southwestern Ireland.

I set out very early on my first morning in Killarney, first stopping for breakfast at a small restaurant on the high street. There, I met a lovely, very elderly, local gentleman who seemed a bit concerned when I excitedly shared my plan for the day. He grumbled sternly: "You'll be travelin' alone in the mist!" He shook his head and strongly advised me to reschedule. Since I've made it a habit during my travels to listen mindfully to local knowledge and advice, I waited and spent the day wandering the high street instead. The next morning, I took off again and, indeed, it was a much clearer day.

Once on the Ring proper, I made a lot of stops to take photos, admire the view, and breathe in the indescribable fragrance. At one of my stops, I noticed a small gap in the parapet of a bridge that crossed over a fast-moving stream. I ignored it at first, but it called to me repeatedly, and I felt compelled to find out what was on the other side. No one was around, no cars had passed since I had parked, so I grabbed my small backpack, some water, and my cane, and walked across the bridge.

On reaching the gap, I peered over the edge to find a very steep flight of moss-covered steps. I picked my way down using my cane for balance and, on reaching the bottom, felt the modern world disappear in a big whoosh. The air was thick with birdsong and a peaty aroma, the stream was rushing, the ground crunched with leaves as I slowly made my way. A large tree with a big rock beneath it caught my eye. I wandered over and took a seat to balance myself and snap some pictures. The nature sounds were like a lullaby. I set my gear aside, got comfortable, and leaned back into the tree. I felt myself being lulled into that particular place of wakeful sleeping. I was slightly alarmed when I felt unable to stop my descent, but it somehow came to my mind that I was safe, and my fear quickly dissipated.

I am still not fully aware of all that happened during my time in that space, only that hours had passed between me taking the steps down into the green and then coming back fully into myself. I do recall wandering to the water's edge and dipping my feet into the cool rushing stream. I took pictures of the moss and the small pools of clear water under the trees. I didn't see the bridge anymore, nor the church on the road above the stream. I knew I'd somehow slipped into another place. I could feel Brigid with me there. It was enchanting; it was peaceful.

While I was there, I realized that these gossamer spaces—the spots where the veil is thin and you can move between worlds—exist all over Mother Earth so her children can spend time in the arms of the goddess. In that green, fragrant, thin space, as I felt Brigid's presence—the coolness of her sacred water, healing in so many ways—I suddenly knew that the answer to my father's paternity lay with an Irish-descended family whose surname's significance to me would become clear the moment I heard it. I only had to trust that the answers would come in their own time.

The rest of my day was wonderful, despite my feeling unwell. I didn't realize it at the time, but I was already carrying the dangerous blood clots in my legs that would soon break off and travel to my lungs. I became very sick during my last days in Ireland, my heart pounding and my breath short, but I presumed it was a virulent respiratory bug of some sort. I made my way back to England, to Glastonbury and Chalice Well, before boarding my ship for home. I was afraid of being sick in a foreign country with no family around and so refused to admit to myself that I was terribly ill. On one of my last days, I found myself at Chalice Well, standing in the healing water with its icy cold flowing over my feet and ankles. Again, I felt Brigid with me. I prayed there, tears rolling down my face, and asked to be kept safe until I made my way home.

I was very sick on board ship and, for most of the crossing, I stayed in my stateroom—with one exception. I rose before dawn to watch the Statue of Liberty come into view as we entered New York Harbor. As we approached, hundreds and hundreds of people leaned over the rails; a feeling of excitement filled the air. I thought of all my ancestors who had braved an ocean crossing in search of a better life. I could feel their essence within me, and tears streamed down my face as I imagined their hearts as they sailed into the New World to begin again.

I flew from New York to New Orleans and was extremely ill on the flight. Upon arriving home, I felt worse. My husband brought me to the hospital, where I was diagnosed with deep vein thrombosis and pulmonary embolism. I was in heart failure and was given an intravenous blood thinner and other medications to stabilize me. My cardiologist told me that I'd had a "saddle embolism," which occurs when a large blood clot in the leg breaks free, travels up and through the heart, and gets stuck where the big vessels split between the lungs. Normally, this stops blood flow to the lungs, which stops oxygen exchange, which causes people to drop dead. He said I certainly should not have survived the initial breaking off of the clot, and most certainly the plane ride between New York City and New Orleans should've been my end. "You obviously have more to do here," he said, looking at me pointedly. Then he left me to consider exactly what that might be.

The next few years were spent in a complicated recovery. I was constantly short of breath and simple tasks like showering left me exhausted and unable to do more than sit. I had to rely on my family to organize and run my event, the New Orleans Witch's Ball. I descended into a deep depression that was made worse by anxiety and panic attacks fueled by the terror that I would get another clot and drop dead in a gasping heap. Friends who were dear to me, and to whom I thought I was also dear, disappeared, unable to cope with the fun-crushing aftereffects of my illness and the unpredictable upwelling of my fear. It was a dark time in my life and I clung to Brigid. I kept to quiet activities and worked on my father's genealogy mystery. Eventually, the love of my family, close friends, therapy, and a support group lifted me up and into a place where I could begin to live again more fully.

In early 2018, after years of effort, I finally got a DNA match for my father that brought me to the surname Carroll. As told to me on the Ring of Kerry, this name is very powerful and significant for me. My mother and I share a double middle name—Carol Elizabeth—and my own chosen magical name of Cairelle is based on, and pronounced the same as, Carol. The three names—Carol, Cairelle, Carroll—are identical in sound and create a triplicity that speaks to my heart as a magical woman and goddess priestess. After more research, I determined that my father's father was a WWII soldier named John Carroll. John's paternal grandparents were Irish. They came from Ireland at the height of *An Gorta Mór*, the Great Hunger. This information came to me all at once and the serendipity of it was not lost on me. My sister's intense pull to Ireland was grounded in genetic memory; my own experiences while there, and in Cornwall and Wales, came from deep within my own bones and blood.

In the summer of 2018, I was finally well enough to travel again. I brought a dear friend to Scotland, the birthplace of her father. She was very emotional; she cried and shared that a deep yearning in her soul had been filled by the visit. After we explored Scotland a bit, I made my way back down to Chalice Well. I stood in the red water that flowed icy cold over my ankles, and I cried in gratitude for still being alive, for finding my deeper connection to Brigid, and for the ease in heartache related to my father by the discovery of our Carroll ancestors.

In talking with many other women, I find it is often the case that we don't know what we don't know until we set foot onto the soil that carries the blood, sweat, and tears of our ancestors. I am American first, my culture and experiences shaped by this land to which my ancestors traveled to build a new life. But I cannot help feeling a deep and abiding connection to the faraway places they once called home. In some ways, those lands are home for me too.

I hope to return soon. I may bring priestess sisters to that secret grove by the rushing stream. Or perhaps I will take a side trip alone, nestle myself into that rock and tree, and sink once again into the mists of magic and timelessness in the land I can feel in my bones, cradled by Brigid's healing love. In Ireland, it is said the gods and goddesses are the ancestors of the people. Therefore, Brigid is my ancestor and I am her daughter.

This is what I know to be true.

Conclusion

The persistence of Brigid's faithful in the modern world speaks to the resilience of this ancient goddess. Just as the flame of devotion to her was carried within countless hearts from beloved homelands toward opportunity and hope for a better future, so too does her voice continue to reverberate in the stories, art, food, folklore, rituals, and magic of her tradition. This anthology aims to let that voice be heard.

Our experiences with and our understanding of this enigmatic goddess are as dissimilar as our fingerprints. But, with each turn of the Wheel of Life, Brigid reveals the tools we each need to meet the challenges of life, to revel in its beauty, and to enjoy its gifts. She stands at the center, the hearth, bringing light and warmth to all. With her gentle nature, she calls to us and woos us with her tender heart. She meets us where we are. With her strength, she inspires us to be and to do, and to provide an example for those who follow. She travels with us as we wander, pointing out the power of the dawn.

When we journey in pilgrimage to the holy places of our origin, perhaps we fulfill a longing of the soul to plunge our hands into the earth and physically bond with it, adding its essence to our being. The bones and the blood remember. Despite this divine connection to the past, however, we also stand tall as modern reflections of the patchwork that is our heritage. We are a coincidental collective, linked by the circumstances of our birth. We respect the ways of old, even as we simultaneously speak with a unique voice born from the past and transformed into a beauty that is all our own.

The tradition of keeping a flame for Brigid is an old one, with roots that hearken back to a story of nineteen priestesses tending a perpetual flame for her in Kildare. Even in modern times, flames flicker in the darkness for this goddess and saint every night of the year, kept alight by devotees from all walks of life and a variety of spiritual traditions. We leave you with this prayer, intended for such a vigil. It was written over shared cups of tea and tales of ancestors, and is infused with our deep love of the goddess. May it bring you bright blessings.

Brigid, O Exalted One,
In devotion, I light this flame.
With gratitude and a happy heart,
I bid you welcome to this holy space.

Brigid of the Hearth Fire,
Keep my home free from negativity and harm,
And may all who enter here with good intent
Be blessed with the abundance of enough.

Brigid of Kith and Kin,
Surround my beloveds, those by blood and by bond,
With an endless bounty of all that is needed, and
May they always feel cherished beyond measure.

Brigid of the Sacred Well,
I pray for the blessings of your holy water to mend me,
Keep me in my best health and offer comfort and ease to those in
    need.
May the hands and minds of all healers be guided by your wisdom.

Brigid of the Red Tent,
Walk with me as I journey through these luscious years of woman-
    hood,
Encourage me to sing loudly in praise of my body's sovereignty and
    power,
My womb space ever humming the genetic melody passed down
    through the millennia by the ancient Mothers.

Brigid of the Grateful Heart,
In this moment, may I feel appreciation for each breath, in and out,
    that sustains me.
Let the rising sun at dawn, every fiery sunset, remind me daily: "I am
    still here."
Open my eyes to each blessing, that I may feel deeply thankful for all
    that I have.

Brigid of the Mighty Oak,
Let me never forget that I am a woman of sovereignty and great
    strength,
To always remember with clarity my purpose, that I may overcome
    all challenges
With fortitude, grace, respect for others, and a sense of accomplish-
    ment.

Brigid of the Open Mind,
May my eyes see clearly the struggles of others and
My thoughts and words keep free of judgment as
I walk this life's path with compassion for all beings.

Brigid of the Bees,
Cause the buzz of empty words and gossip to stay far from my ears,
And the love and support of true friends be well-known to my heart.
May I strive always to uplift the sisters of my soul toward their high-
    est potential.

Brigid of the Bountiful Garden,
Help me to find all that I need, remind me when I have enough.
May I be strong and focused as I sow the seeds that will
Manifest a heart-filling, plentiful harvest of blessings.

Brigid, O Inspiratrix,
Bless the needle of my imagination, weave my thoughts into
Binding threads that manifest tapestries of meaningful beauty.
May your bubbling cauldron of creativity continue to inspire me.

Brigid of the Keening,
The world is filled with pain and loss, so many are burdened with
    sadness.
I pray to you, send a balm to soothe the hearts of the grieving,
Drape over them the mantle of your love, that comfort and ease may
    be found within.

Brigid of the Passionate Heart,
May the fire of devotion burn ever bright, a beacon to remind me of
    delight.

I pray for a true and lasting bond, one that nurtures and honors,
A boundless love that fills the hours and days and years with joy and
laughter.

Brigid of Inner Knowing,
Shine your light on what I have not examined so that I will act and
speak with awareness.
Lift all veils of deception and obscurity as I seek knowledge of the
truths at hand.
Open my mind fully so I see and feel what is hidden, and may I
always trust my own judgment.

Brigid of the Sacred Ways,
Inspire me with words of wisdom, open my heart to the path of my
highest good.
In sovereignty and grace, may I flourish in my dedication to you.
As I journey through life, I pray my words and actions are of benefit
to all beings.

Brigid of Ancestral Connection,
My Beloved Dead speak with every beat of my heart. I am them, and
they are me.
Their echoes in my blood encourage me to acknowledge the past and
to honor what is honorable.
May I always walk the path of right action to adjust and heal my
lineage for the highest good.

Brigid of Selfless Service,
I pray to always be fully aware and mindful of those who have need.
Keep within me the passion to be a force of good in the world,
May my works be a genuine and fragrant offering from my heart.

Brigid, Beacon of Integrity,
Hold high your flame and illuminate the treacherous path of injus-
tice,
Bring truth to awareness, lift our voices to speak for those unable.
Balance the scales, open hearts and minds, that all who seek justness
receive it.

Brigid of the Diaspora,
I am a descendant of your traveling children, living far from the
lands of my ancestors.
I speak your name in devotion and pray for love, health, prosperity,
and happiness.
As deeply as I feel you in the marrow of my bones, so too may I be
blessed by your light.

List of Illustrations

Part I
Figure 1. Celtic Cross. Photo by Linda L. Minutola.
Figure 2. The Goddess Brigit. Photo by Sandra Román.
Figure 3. *Holy Brighid Holding the World in Her Hands.* Painting by Rev. Rowan Fairgrove
Figure 4. Francis J. "Frank" McCabe. Photo from Gera Clark.

Part II
Figure 5. Brigid and the King's Wolf. Pendant by Val Damon and Jean Hendon. Photo by Paul Lindholm.
Figure 6. *Brigid's Fire.* Drawing by Laura Tempest Zakroff.
Figure 7. *Brigid of the Oak.* Hand-pulled linocut print by Holly Devanna.
Figure 8. *Juncus effusus.* Painting by J. Ellen Cooper.

Part III
Figure 9. *Brigid of Kildare.* Drawing by Sierra Linder.
Figure 10. Walking Brigid's Path tarot spread. Picture by Nancy Hendrickson.
Figure 11. *Light Anchoring.* Photo by Chantal Simon.

Part IV
Figure 12. Makings of an Imbolc feast for Brigid. Photo by Dawn Aurora Hunt.

Part V
Figure 13. The Fleming Sisters. Photo from the collection of Brigid Marie Bennett.
Figure 14. *Brigid of Healing.* Painting by Nic Phillips.
Figure 15. *Brigantia,* protector goddess and healer. Painting by Marion Brigantia van Eupen.
Figure 16. Brigid's quilts. Photo by Laura Louella.
Figure 17. Jane Victoria Bridwell Kilpatrick. Photo from the collection of Laura Louella.

Part VI
Figure 18. *She Who Dwells Between the Worlds.* Photo by Chantal Simon.
Figure 19. *Maman Brijit.* Painting by Raven Morgaine.

About the Editors

Cairelle Crow, a descendant of James Carroll and Cecelia Dora O'Heron Carroll of Ireland, has walked a goddess path for more than thirty years, exploring, learning, and growing. She is a priestess, genealogist, wanderess of wild and holy places, and cofoundress of the Sanctuary of Brigid and its flame-keeping *cill*, Sisters of the Flame. She lectures locally, nationally, and internationally on the blending of genealogy with magic and, through her company Sacred Roots, is dedicated to connecting magical people to their ancestral truths. She also organizes Divine You retreats that introduce magical women to sacred travel experiences. When she's not roaming the world in search of grandmothers, quirky art, and stone circles, Cairelle is home in New Orleans, where she lives joyfully, loves intensely, and laughs frequently with beloved family and friends. You can find her online at *www.cairellecrow.com*.

Laura Louella is a descendant of Catherine MacKenzie of Scotland and of James Robert Kilpatrick and Jane Victoria Bridwell Kilpatrick, whose ancestors hail from Ireland and England. For many years, Laura chose a solitary path. Always an information gatherer, she read, and read, and read some more. When the time was right, she began training with a group of women who supported and challenged her to dream big and follow the thread. She is a priestess, certified Pilates instructor committed to teaching the strength that lies within, and the owner of Goddess Pilates, where she blends the art of sacred movement with the beauty of the goddess. She is also the cofoundress of the Sanctuary of Brigid and its flame-keeping *cill*, Sisters of the Flame. Many days, you can find her tending her garden, taking long walks through the forest, sitting by the river, or creating a quilt on her 1936 Featherweight Singer sewing machine. Laura lives in the Cascade Mountains of northern California.

The Contributors

Tara Anura, a descendant of Lois, is a curvy mystic and a museum, movie, nature, and book lover who lives with her dog in a humble hovel on the Ozark plateau. She's been taught by many women, both living and those who are the Beloved Dead, in person and through their writing. She has been a priestess for more than twenty years. Part of her priestess work is to honor past, present, and future words by women, for women. She is the hostess of the Hypatia literary group on Facebook, and she interviews women authors and leaders on the Hypatia podcast on YouTube. She earns her keep by weaving children's stories at the local library.

Annwyn Avalon, daughter of Ruth Edgington Hughes of Birmingham, England, and granddaughter of Roy Edgington of Knowles, England, is a water witch and water priestess, and the founder of Triskele Rose Witchcraft, an Avalonian witchcraft tradition. She has devoted her life to the study of art, witchcraft, and magic. She is an initiated witch and priestess, Reiki master teacher, award-winning dancer, and published author. She holds a BFA in sculpture and a BA in anthropology with emphasis on plant and human interactions. She has also received an apprentice certificate in herbalism. She writes for *The Magical Times* magazine in the UK and has contributed to other published works like *The New Aradia: A Witch's Handbook to Magical Resistance*. She is the author of *Water Witchcraft: Magic and Lore from the Celtic Tradition* and *The Way of the Water Priestess: Entering the World of Water Magic*. Visit her at *www.WaterWitchcraft.com*, *www.WaterPriestess.com*, and *www.TriskeleRose.com*.

H. Byron Ballard, BA, MFA, is a descendant of Mary Marie Helm Robeson of Scotland and Andrew Robeson of Pennsylvania. She is a native of western North Carolina, where she is a teacher, a folklorist, and a writer. She has served as a featured speaker and teacher at festivals and conferences in the United States and the UK. Her essays are featured in several anthologies and she writes a regular column for *SageWoman* magazine. Her books include *Staubs and Ditchwater, Asfidity and Mad-Stones, Embracing Willendorf, Earth Works: Ceremonies in Tower Time, Roots, Branches, and Spirits,* and *Seasons of a Magical Life: a Pagan Path of Living.* You can find her online at *www.myvillagewitch.com.*

Brigid Marie Bennett, a descendant of Josephine Fleming of Ireland, is a mother, small business owner, nurse, silversmith apprentice, and artist from Upstate New York. You can find her work in her online shop, Goddess Grown, at *www.etsy.com.*

Amy Blackthorn, a descendant of Betty Parker Rose of Ireland, is the best-selling author of *Blackthorn's Botanical Magic, Sacred Smoke,* and *Blackthorn's Botanical Brews.* She has been described as an "arcane horticulturalist" for her lifelong work with magical plants and teaching. She integrates her experiences in British Traditional Witchcraft with her horticulture studies. She has a certification in aromatherapy and is an ordained priestess through the Order of the Golden Gryphon. Amy's company, Blackthorns Botanicals, creates teas based on magical associations. She has appeared on HuffPoLive, Netflix's *Top Ten Secrets and Mysteries* in an episode about supernatural abilities, and the Associated Press' *Newswire.* Amy lives in Delaware. You can view Amy's tea shop at *Blackthornsbotanicals.com.*

Marion Brigantia van Eupen, a maternal line descendant of Antonia Rombouts, Anna Calis, and Anna Coletha Giclens of The Netherlands, is a Priestess of Brighde-Brigantia and of Avalon. Marion reclaims, celebrates, and serves the goddess as a priestess every day of her life. She holds many strands of priestess work, with a big emphasis on the Brighde-Brigantia teachings, of which she is the founder and tutor. This priest/ess training is taught internationally, online and in-person, by tutors trained by Marion. She is also the co-organizer of the annual Goddess Conference in Glastonbury. Her priestess work also includes sacred tours and walks on the land, ceremonies, workshops, oracle readings, shamanic drumming, healing, and soul work. Learn more about Marion at *www.marionbrigantia.com.*

Mael Brigde, a descendant of Sarah Blythe of Saint Margaret's, County Dublin, Ireland, and Christina McVicar of North Uist, Hebrides, Scotland, is a devotee of the Irish goddess and saint, Brigit, and the founder of Daughters of the Flame, a group that has tended Brigit's flame since Imbolc 1993. She publishes a general-interest Brigit blog, *Brigit's Sparkling Flame*, and a Brigit poetry blog, *Stone on the Belly*. She teaches courses and webinars on Brigit, including Journey with Brigit, Goddess of Poetry, an intensive class that explores reading and writing poetry as a sacred act. She is the author of *A Brigit of Ireland Devotional: Sun Among Stars*. Mael Brigde lives in Vancouver, Canada.

Rev. Angie Buchanan is an animist family-tradition Pagan. She is the cofounder and the spiritual director of Earth Traditions, a Pagan church. In 2011, after a lifetime of experience in the birth and death thresholds, she became a certified death midwife under Nora Cedarwind Young. In 2014, she was certified to teach. She developed and currently teaches internationally a certification course that provides hands-on, intensive training for compassionate end-of-life care and information on ecologically sensitive funerals. She also holds separate psychopomp workshops that address the psycho-spiritual aspects of death and dying. She resides in the American Midwest. You can find her online at *www.DeathMidwife.org* and *www.EarthTraditions.org*.

Kelly Jo Carroll, a descendant of Hugh Rowan and Mary Meehan Rowan of Ireland, is an acrylic artist who works with differently abled children. Her Sun sign of Taurus is ever apparent as she cultivates her connection with the earth by growing herbs and communing with Mother Nature while walking in the bayous and marshes near her home. She lives in southeastern Louisiana with her seventeen-year-old cat, Yuna.

Gera Clark, a descendant of Francis McCabe and Susan Conboy McCabe of Ireland, is a New Age composer, instrumentalist, and performer. She plays Native American flutes with Celtic instruments, weaving a gorgeous tapestry of sound intended to heal. Gera, a holistic nurse, yoga and meditation teacher, and herbalist, writes reflections that allow readers to see the beauty in this life. You can find her online at *www.geraclark.com*.

J. Ellen Cooper, a descendant of Martin Finnegan of Ireland and Ellen Robertson of Scotland, is an ecologist, artist, writer, and mother living on the shore of Sydney Harbor. Blending art and science, she focuses on our world through a lens trained on the web between the details. Her artworks are held together with screws and wires harvested from expired objects, because science holds wonder, but also truth—a piece that diverts waste seems to be more honest. Delighting in anarchy, Cooper transcends pigeonholes by using art to explore biology and imagination to inspire scientific understanding.

Val Damon was born and bred in New York City and is currently crafting jewelry in Brooklyn following a stay in Arizona to obtain a master's in art and visual culture. She has exhibited and sold work at galleries and museum shops nationally and has participated in numerous juried exhibitions and shows, including American Craft Council events. Her mother, Jean Gryzlo Hendon, attended the Fashion Institute of Technology and Parsons School of Design/The New School in New York City. She has exhibited and sold her paintings through galleries in the South and Southwest, including multiple exhibitions at the Tucson Museum of Art.

Jamie Della follows a whimsical path of magick, the swirling of words, and the spinning of stoneware. She is an ordained priestess, hearth witch, creativity mentor, and author of nine published books as well as an herbal journeys blog, *Backside of the Wind*. She has published several essays and poems. You can find her online at *www.jamiedellawrites.com*.

Holly Devanna, a descendant of Henry Chevers and Catherine Fitzwilliam Chevers of Ireland, is an ordained priestess of the Mt. Shasta Goddess Temple, artist, divinatrix, and sacred maker with a lifelong passion for the magical. She's been creating sacred art in various media for decades—hand-printed linocut icons, original hex signs, painted goddesses, and self-published tarot and oracle decks, including *The Incidental Tarot* (2012) and *A Curious Oracle* (2015). She owns a jewelry company with her husband called Forge and Fountain, where they create sacred adornments with an aesthetic of beauty, mythos, and magic. You can see her creations at *www.forgeandfountain.com* and *www.wildempressmagic.com*.

Diane DiPietro is a Massachusetts witch who has been a devotee of Brid for more than twenty years. She and her husband, Patrick, run a metaphysical flower shop called Tintagel's Gate in Athol, Massachusetts, where Diane does psychic readings and energy work. Pat and Diane also facilitate a Celtic Avalonian coven and run open rituals in north-central Massachusetts. Visit her at *www.daughterofbride.com*.

Mary-Grace Fahrun, a descendant of Suor Carla Roselli and Palmina Smarrelli of Italy, was born in Bridgeport, Connecticut, to Italian immigrant parents and grew up in the Italian neighborhoods of Montreal and Connecticut. She describes herself as "an avid keeper of customs, traditions, and secrets," and is an authority on Italian folk magic and folk healing traditions. She is the author of *Italian Folk Magic: Rue's Kitchen Witchery*. Visit her at *www.rueskitchen.com*.

Rev. Rowan Fairgrove, EPs, a descendant of William Gregg and Anne Wilkinson Gregg of Ireland, is a Daughter of the Flame and an FOI-ordained priestess of Brighid. She resonates with Brighid's aspects of healing, transformation, and inspiration. She invokes the goddess when she paints, heals, and works for peace in the world. Rowan has carried the holy flame of Brighid and shared it on three continents, including offering a Brighid meditation at the Parliament of the World's Religions in Cape Town in 1999.

Donna Gerrard, a descendant of Dorothy Innes and Mary Walshaw, is an initiated Priestess of Brighde-Brigantia, and of the Rose lineage in the Avalonian traditions. She is also initiated into the ancient lineages of the Sacred Bee. Donna is a poet and a longtime practitioner and teacher of yoga. Her classes often interweave poetry and the spirituality of these other ancient traditions with that of yoga, in a way that passionately communicates the transformative power of these ancient goddess traditions in a modern context. Learn more about Donna at *www.donnagerrard.com*.

Nancy Hendrickson, a descendant of Marjorie Dearing Goodwine of England, is the author of *Ancestral Tarot*. She works with tarot, pendulums, and polished-stone castings on her journey to find guidance and support from the ancestral realm. Her latest book, *Ancestral Magic*, will be published in autumn 2022. In it, readers will take a deep dive into the lives of their magical ancestors, creating a personalized guide to their own magical lives. Nancy is active on Instagram (@nancysageshadow) and on her website (*SageandShadow.com*). You can find her on IG Live doing readings at significant times of the year, like the Day of the Dead and Lammas. Nancy currently lives in San Diego, California, and enjoys traveling to ancient sites in the Southwest.

Dawn Aurora Hunt, known as "the kitchen witch," is the owner and CEO of Cucina Aurora Kitchen Witchery. She has been teaching and writing on the topics of kitchen witchery and spiritual nutrition since 2010, when she started her own company making gourmet foods with a dash of magic and a heaping helping of positive vibes as the main ingredients. With simple ingredients and the power of intention, Dawn teaches people how to cook simple meals in a mindful and magical way to help achieve spiritual goals. Incorporating magic and energy work into food, she has grown her brand to reach people from all faiths and spiritual backgrounds. The author of *Tastes from the Temple* (Copper Cauldron LLC) and *A Kitchen Witch's Guide to Recipes for Love & Romance* (Tiller Press Simon & Schuster), Dawn speaks at events all along the East Coast and appears regularly on local TV, teaching people that, with a little intention and a lot of love, cooking and kitchen witchery can be an easy way to practice your craft every day. Find her online at *www.cucinaaurora.com*.

Kelley Eileen Ingols is a lover of the land and wild nature. She is an educator, mother, priestess, and creatrix who inspires others to tap into their inner and outer landscapes. She cocreates opportunities to be in the flow and rhythms of the year through offerings and ceremonies. Kelley was initiated as Bhrida Morgana many years ago when she answered the call to step onto the priestess path with Holly Rhiannon and the Awakening Avalon Temple. Brigid/Bhrida has ignited her to be of service to the lineage and to journey this earth, walking with the flow and inspiration that arise to share.

Karol Jackowski entered the sisterhood in 1964 and is currently a member of the Sisters for Christian Community. A native of East Chicago, Indiana, Karol lives now and forever in New York City, where she works as a writer. She teaches graduate writing classes at Bay Path University in Longmeadow, Massachusetts. Karol has published eight books to date, including the best-selling *Ten Fun Things To Do Before You Die* and *Sister Karol's Book of Spells, Blessings, and Folk Magic*. In reflecting on the path her life has taken, Karol says: "I stand on the shoulders of Brigid and all women who walk in the footsteps of the goddess."

Maria Jones, a descendant of Jane Edwards Dorrell and Gordon Dorrell of England, is an initiated Priestess of Avalon and the creatrix of the Silver Spiral of Goddess Astrology teachings. She is deeply devoted to bringing back the ancient feminine mysteries and awakening the memory of our Great Cosmic Mother. Her work is designed to weave together the astrological cycles of the cosmos and seasonal movements of the earth, which are intimately entwined and profoundly affect us on all levels. Maria's intention is to help support those who connect with her teachings, readings, and offerings to realign themselves with this inner knowing in ways that create transformation, healing, and radical self-acceptance. Find her online at *www.inspirationsforyourjourneybacktoavalon.com*.

Sierra Linder, a descendant of John MacDonald and Anna Forbes MacDonald of Scotland, is a twenty-one-year-old artist and college student from southeastern Louisiana. She has an affinity for cats and prefers warmer temperatures and rain.

Holly V. MacKenna, MD, is a descendant of Bridie Bray and Jarlath MacKenna of Ireland. She is a board-certified psychiatrist who has been in practice for over twenty years. She is fellowship-trained in Integrative Medicine and specializes in providing whole-person care to those who have experienced psychological trauma and traumatic brain injuries. Dr. MacKenna comes from a long line of educators and healers dating back centuries in Ireland. Her father's people migrated to County Kildare before he was born and are now buried in his hometown of Castledermot. She honors their memory and spirit in her daily practice. She named her private medical clinic Dara as a nod to *Cill Dara* (Kildare). Find her online at *www.darawellnessnola.com*.

Yeshe Matthews is the great-granddaughter of James Coleman, whose parents hailed from England and Ireland. She is the Mandala Priestess of the Mt. Shasta Goddess Temple, a dharma practitioner, and co-owner of The Sacred Well shop, a metaphysical boutique in Dunsmuir, California. You can find her on the Goddess Temple app, as well as on Facebook and Instagram, as Priestess Yeshe, or on TikTok (@mtshastagoddess). Find her online at *www.mtshastagoddesstemple.com* and *www.sacredwell.com*.

Jenne Micale is a writer, singer, priestess, and musician whose endeavors include the ethereal/wyrd music project Kwannon and the wyrd folk band formerly known as Belladonna Bouquet. Her work has appeared in *Enheduenna, Mandragora, Oak Leaves, Keltria: Journal of Druidism and Magic,* and the anthologies *Talking About the Elephant, To Fly By Night: An Anthology of Hedgewitchery and Brighid,* and *Me: Experiences with the Goddess.* A member of *Ár nDraíocht Féin* and the Sisterhood of Avalon, she has a PhD in English literature and lives with her husband and cat in the wilds surrounding Binghamton, New York. Visit her online at *www.kwannon.net*.

Linda L. Minutola, aka Lady Luna Photography, has been living and working in New Orleans since 2008. She is a professional photographer who is known nationally and internationally for her insightful and emotive work photographing New Orleans' iconic and historic imagery through her unique perspective.

Bernadette Montana, a descendant of Giacomina Arra and Modesta Acevedo, grew up in New York City in the 1970s and 1980s, where she immersed herself in the punk music scene of Greenwich Village. After her introduction to Paganism, she was a frequent patron at Enchantments and Magickal Childe. She is a 3rd-degree Priestess of Brid in the lineage of high priestess Janet Farrar and high priest Gavin Bone. Her specializations include tarot, Lenormand, mediumship, spiritual counseling, and teaching. She also hosts an annual Beltane Festival at Palaia Winery in Highland Mills, New York. Bernadette is married, the mother of three sons, and owner of the metaphysical shop Brid's Closet in Cornwall-on-Hudson, New York.

Kimberly Moore, a descendant of Rose O'Neal of Ireland, is the founder and priestess of MotherHouse, an online devotional community and living altar to the goddess in all of her emanations. Through ritual, myth, magick, and sacred inspiration, MotherHouse offers sanctuary for those seeking transformation through the Divine Feminine. Kimberly has been a goddess priestess for more than twenty-five years. Her mission is working with women personally or in groups (professionally and spiritually), crafting soul-speaking rituals, and holding sacred space for women to activate the soul seeds of the goddess within them. She is also an aborisha in Lukumi and a daughter of Oshun.

Lucía Moreno-Velo is a Pagan theology student at Cherry Hill Seminary. She is interested in exploring how the recovery of ancient religions can contribute to social and climate justice for today and tomorrow. Her first sincere prayer in a moment of danger was to Brigid, a goddess she knew only by name at the time. She later discovered that her mother's family came from a village in northwestern Spain named after Brigid. With Gwyneth Box, she co-runs the Modern Pagan Prayers project, an effort to create a contemporary body of texts for use in personal devotion and public ritual. She lives with her wife, two teens, and two cats in the mountains near Madrid, Spain. You can find her online at *www.modernpaganprayers.com*.

Raven Morgaine is a spiritual artist who has dedicated his life and work to the service of the great mother goddess, Yemaya. A practitioner of Candomblé, New Orleans Voodoo, Santeria, and witchcraft, he is the owner of the Familiar Spirits shop where he creates and sells the spirit altar dolls for which he is renowned. He has been featured in numerous publications and podcasts. Raven lives in Rhode Island.

Carole Murray (1949–2018), astrologer, tarotista, altar builder, writer, poet, and passionate cook was a longtime, flame-keeper for Brigid. She was a tarot artist whose card images appear in *The Encyclopedia of Tarot, Volume III* (US Games, 1990). A lover of New Orleans, she lived and worked in New York City.

NíDara is a poet, artist, and flametender of Brighid. She combines her immense love of researching myth and folklore with experiential mysticism to develop her spiritual path. NíDara lives in Texas.

M. A. Phillips, a descendant of Mary Moran of Ireland, is an author who lives in northern New York with her husband, daughter, and two cats. She is an English teacher and senior Druid of Northern Rivers Grove, ADF. Her religion and region inspire much of her writing. Her work has appeared in the Pagan magazines *Oak Leaves* and *Stone, Root, and Bone*. She is the author of the magical realism series *Rituals of Rock Bay* (Shadow Spark Publishing) and of a novel entitled *Forest Magic* (2021). You can read more about her spiritual and creative journey at *ditzydruid.com* and on Instagram @ditzydruid.

Nic Phillips lives in the UK, where he creates sacred, largely goddess-orientated art. He is the artist behind *Pistis Sophia: The Goddess Tarot* and *Sol Invictus: The God Tarot* (Schiffer) and the author of *Breaking Chains: The Evolution of the Black Madonna* and *Celtic Saints of Western Britain* (Avalonia).

Sandra Román is a priestess, ceremonialist, writer, teacher, sacred singer, tarot reader, past-lives therapist, and Kundalini yoga instructor. She worked as a journalist until the call of the goddess brought her to Glastonbury, where she was trained as a Priestess of Avalon. She was initiated at Chalice Well on the autumn equinox in 2000. Sandra teaches goddess trainings in South America, Mexico, and Spain. Inspired by her service as a Melissa at the Glastonbury Goddess Temple, she founded the first Argentinian Goddess Temple in Capilla del Monte, Argentina, a powerful sacred place in the province of Cordoba. She also organized the first Argentinian Goddess Conference. You can find Sandra online at *www.losrostrosdeladiosa.com*.

Michael Routery, a descendant of James Walsh and Brigit O'Hara Walsh of Ireland, is a poet, teacher, writer, and Druid who follows Celtic polytheistic pathways and has long been devoted to Brigid. Originally from California, they currently live in the middle of the Pacific Ocean on Hawai'i, on a steep green height above a rushing stream. More of Michael's writing can be found in their book of devotional poetry *From the Prow of Myth* and on the blog *Finnchuill's Mast*, as well as in numerous anthologies.

Annie Russell, a descendant of Malcolm Campbell and Anna Anderson Campbell of Scotland, is an author, chef, and artist who splits her time between New Orleans and Charlevoix, Michigan. She combines her talents into unique tales of her most beloved locations and incorporates the smells, tastes, and colors of each by utilizing words, original art, and recipes to bring her world to life for her readers. Visit *www.annierussell.net* to learn more about her writing, cooking, and art.

Lynne Sedgmore, CBE, DProf, is a descendant of Alice Vera Jones Sedgmore and Margaret Jane Angel. She is a Priestess of Avalon, poetess, retired chief executive, soul coach, and priestess healer. She lives in Glastonbury, UK. Her three poetry collections are *Enlivenment* (Chrysalis Press 2013), *Healing through the Goddess* (TheaSpeaks Press 2017), and *Crone* (TheaSpeaks Press 2019). She is founder of and tutor for the Goddess Luminary Wheel trainings, a unique combination of liberating leadership, feminism, and goddess spirituality offered through the Glastonbury Goddess Temple. She is of Cornish and Welsh lineage and steeped in the Celtic and Avalonian goddess traditions. She has three daughters and two granddaughters.

Chantal Simon is a writer, translator, and photographer of Breton heritage living on the northwest coast of Ireland. As well as working on a memoir about her spiritual unfolding, she is currently creating a photographic series inspired by her natural surroundings and her love of the liminal.

Jim "Raven" Stefanowicz, a descendant of Hercules Russell and Mary Murray Russell of Ireland, is a Pagan priest and tarot reader based in

Philadelphia, Pennsylvania. He is the founder and high priest of the South Street Circle, a Pagan ritual group, and is also a 2nd-degree initiate in the Cabot tradition.

Jennifer Sundeen, a descendant of Sir James McKee of Scotland and Mary Hutchison of Scotland, is a spiritual teacher, writer, activist, community architect, nature lover, and the mother of three daughters. She is the founder of several organizations that support girls, women, spirituality, and the earth, including the Durga Studio, Durga's Red Tent, and Goddess Pilgrimages. Jennifer recently published her translations of the Kashmiri poetess Lalla, *Lalla Unveiled: The Naked Voice of the Feminine,* and is currently pursuing her doctorate in earth ministry. If she isn't exploring ancient goddess temples, she can be found back home in the woods of New England, hiking with her dog, Harley, and hanging with the trees. Learn more about Jennifer at *www.jennifersundeen.com.*

Rowan Taw, a descendant of Geneverah Blake and Bryant Kempton of England, is a poet whose name reveals her connection to the land, to people, and to time. "Rowan" speaks of the trees found beside her home on the River Taw in Devon, England. Her maternal roots are still there in North Devon, as well as in Wiltshire, the home of Stonehenge, where her paternal connection lies. Those Celtic roots go even deeper, as revealed by DNA that ties her to Scotland, Ireland, and Wales. Rowan is a student of the spiritual path who works in the psychology of mindfulness, meditation, and spirituality. She resides in Auckland, New Zealand.

Rev. Rayna Templebee, a descendant of Agnes Hanny of Ireland and of Marjorie Lambert Risser, is a daughter of the Ocean Mother and High Priestess of Beachfyre Coven in Miami, Florida. She holds ministerial credentials through the Covenant of the Goddess and offers rites of passage to queer, polyamorous, and other freethinking Pagans. Rayna was raised in a family that spoke with plants and was initiated as a witch in 1983. She is a faery seer and member of Orion Foxwood's House of Brigh, as well as a member of the Mt. Shasta Goddess Temple. Learn more about her spiritual practice and teaching at *www.raynatemplebee.com.*

Mary Tidbury is a Bridget priestess, trained in Glastonbury, England. She assisted with training during her first two years of study and was dedicated as Priestess of Brigantia after the third year. She is part of two flame-keeping circles. Her ancestors hail from the northeast of Ireland and the southwest of Scotland, the Dalriada. She is a retired teacher who now spends her time walking, writing, praying, and learning. She lives in beautiful Somerset.

Courtney Weber is a witch, author, and tarot advisor. She is the author of *Brigid: History, Mystery, and Magick of the Celtic Goddess; Tarot for One: The Art of Reading For Yourself; The Morrigan: Celtic Goddess of Magick and Might;* and *Hekate: Goddess of Witches*. She produced and designed the now-cult classic *Tarot of the Boroughs*. She is a cohost of *That Witch Life* podcast and lives with her husband and pack of rescued critters in McMinnville, Oregon. Find her online at *courtneyaweber.com*.

Laura Tempest Zakroff is a professional artist, author, dancer, designer, and Modern Traditional Witch based in New England. She holds a BFA from the Rhode Island School of Design and her artwork has received awards and honors worldwide. Her work embodies myth and the esoteric through her drawings and paintings, jewelry, talismans, and other designs. Laura is the author of the best-selling books *Weave the Liminal: Living Modern Traditional Witchcraft* and *Sigil Witchery: A Witch's Guide to Crafting Magick Symbols*, as well as the *Liminal Spirits Oracle* (artist/author) and *Anatomy of a Witch*. Laura edited *The New Aradia: A Witch's Handbook to Magical Resistance* (Revelore Press). She blogs for Patheos as *A Modern Traditional Witch*, contributes to *The Witches' Almanac, Ltd*, and creates the *Witchual Workout* and other programming on her YouTube channel. Laura is the creative force behind several community events and teaches workshops worldwide. Find out more at *www.LauraTempestZakroff.com*.

Acknowledgments

Love, gratitude, and all the best coffee to my husband, Kirk. He gently moves my candle work off our stove so he can cook for me while I do my thing; he carries my boxes; he shows up to all the events without complaint. He has walked with me in faith and (mostly) good cheer for many years now, no matter my endeavor. He is, without a doubt, my biggest fan and the love of my life.

Without the support of my family, I could not do what I do. I am beyond blessed. To my smart, savvy, beautiful daughters who have been there in the ways that matter for every single magical venture of mine, thank you from your Mama. I have the best girls ever. You are my hearts, my most exacting teachers, and my pride and joy. To my grandsons, your GiGi knows you're the best boys in the whole world and I love you as I love no one else. To my mother, I love you, and thank you for always being my loudest cheerleader. To my beautiful Sissy, my confidant and most trustworthy ally since 1970, all my love. Thank you for reminding me time and again that I blaze my own path despite the past.

Christine, you infuriating and amazing Gemini, what can I say? After twenty-five years of talking about it, I'm finally on a shelf. My life is so much better because of your unconditional love and support, although I am still on the bubble about all the advice. Our crazy friendship defies description. To think it all started with a K-Dur mishap! I love you!

Massive kudos and huge thanks to the brilliant Judika Illes for answering a million questions and for patiently midwifing us through the process of birthing this anthology. You are a treasure and I am so glad to call you my friend. To all at Weiser Books who contributed to bringing this project to fruition, I cannot express enough appreciation for each of you. Your professionalism and skill are unparalleled.

I am deeply indebted to my many teachers over the last thirty-plus years. They have all, in their own unique and intentional way, contributed to my lifelong journey. My love of the goddess and this endeavor would not be the same without their wisdom and sharing nature. To those with whom I've circled, past and present, online and in person, my heartfelt gratitude for offering a space of love, encouragement, and acceptance. May we always feel supported and free to speak our truths.

It has been an honor and a privilege to work with the amazing array of talented people who contributed to this anthology. Laura and I shaped this container; you generously filled it with beauty and magic. Thank you for supporting our vision of Brigid with your own.

Laura Louella, coeditor and writing partner extraordinaire, you are the epitome of quiet strength, elegant grace, and heartfelt friendship. Brigid brought us together at just the right time on that dark and stormy night, and this book of devotion is the result. I am excited about our future as we walk this particular path together as priestess sisters, guided by Brigid's light.

Above all, I stand with gratitude before Brigid, Keeper of the Flame, Lady of the Well. I pray her bright light continues to guide me and bless me as I make my way in this crazy beautiful world.

Cairelle Crow

For my family, who may not always understand what I am doing, but who love me through it all. To my mom and grandma, and to all the women before them who carried the flame that led me to Brigid, thank you for showing me what resilience looks like. To my sons, you brought out in me a mother's fierce love. I stand in awe of the wonderful men you have become. Each of you brings me such joy. You are my cubs and there is nothing I wouldn't do for you. My heart is yours.

To my sweet granddaughter, I love you with a love that I did not know was possible. My utmost goal is to teach you that your unique contribution to this world is worth more than the greatest riches. You are pure joy and I am so fortunate to be your Lally.

To Andrew, for your patient acceptance of all it took for me to get here. Your encouragement and love get me through the toughest days.

I am in deep gratitude to my dear friend and priestess sister, Cairelle. For all the time we spent brainstorming, collaborating, laughing, and dreaming about how we would bring Brigid forward and celebrate her, thank you is not enough. Your love of beautiful things, your honesty, and your strength are just a few of the things I admire about you. That you know how all the technology works has been a blessing indeed! I love how we are somehow always on the same page, even though we are far apart. I look forward to where we go from here. May Brigid's flame lead us on great adventures.

To Christine Brusati, my dear friend who makes me laugh and is always ready to listen, thank you for the long walks and for reminding me that there is always hope. You are a wonderful example of fortitude. I appreciate you immensely.

To all of my teachers, I carry a piece of you with me always as I continue to forge my own path. To all the wonderful people I have encountered on this path, may our circle continue to strengthen and grow.

Judika Illes, you took our dream and made it a reality. I appreciate you for seeing the potential and challenging us to do more. Thank you for guiding and encouraging us. To Weiser Books, thank you for saying yes to this honoring of Brigid.

Thanks always to the goddess, who has been calling me since before time, for her patient heart, her love, her strength and tenacity. I am humbled, and I bow down, trusting her to guide me with her light.

Laura

To Our Readers

Weiser Books, an imprint of Red Wheel/Weiser, publishes books across the entire spectrum of occult, esoteric, speculative, and New Age subjects. Our mission is to publish quality books that will make a difference in people's lives without advocating any one particular path or field of study. We value the integrity, originality, and depth of knowledge of our authors.

Our readers are our most important resource, and we appreciate your input, suggestions, and ideas about what you would like to see published.

Visit our website at *www.redwheelweiser.com*, where you can learn about our upcoming books and free downloads, and also find links to sign up for our newsletter and exclusive offers.

You can also contact us at *info@rwwbooks.com* or at
Red Wheel/Weiser, LLC
65 Parker Street, Suite 7
Newburyport, MA 01950